From our Kitchen to Yours

Our Best
Fast, Easy & Delicious
Recipes

Simple and satisfying dinners, sides & desserts ready in a jiffy

To everyone who enjoys great food without the fuss!

Gooseberry Patch
An imprint of Globe Pequot
64 South Main Street
Essex, CT 06426

www.gooseberrypatch.com
1 800 854 6673

••••••••••••••••••••

Do you have a tried & true recipe... tip, craft or memory that you'd like to see featured in a **Gooseberry Patch** cookbook? Visit our website at www.gooseberrypatch.com and follow the easy steps to submit your favorite family recipe.

Or send them to us at:
Gooseberry Patch
PO Box 812
Columbus, OH 43216-0812

Don't forget to include the number of servings your recipe makes, plus your name, address, phone number and email address. If we select your recipe, your name will appear right along with it... and you'll receive a FREE copy of the book!

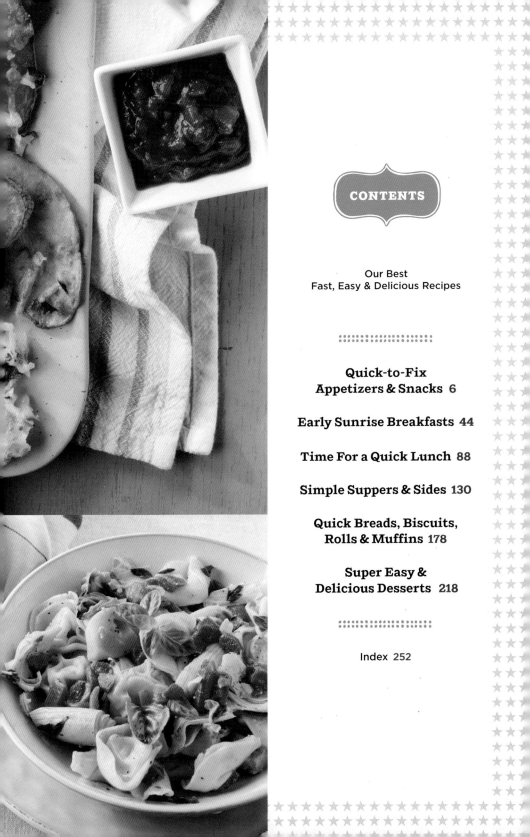

CONTENTS

Our Best
Fast, Easy & Delicious Recipes

::::::::::::::::::::::

Our Best Fast, Easy & Delicious Recipes

Feeling short on time but craving a home-cooked meal? It's easy to get a no-fuss, delicious meal on the table with a few handy tips.

- Read your recipe all the way through before starting. It's tempting to skip this step when you're in a hurry, but making sure you have all of the necessary ingredients before you start cooking is a real time-saver.

- When measuring sticky ingredients like honey or peanut butter, spray the measuring cup with non-stick vegetable spray first. The contents will slip right out, which saves time cleaning up.

- Flexible plastic cutting mats make speedy work of slicing and dicing. Keep two mats on hand, one for chopping veggies and one for meat.

- Use parchment paper to roast all of your veggies. Clean-up is a snap!

- Use already-diced canned and frozen vegetables to make quick work of stir-frys and soups.

- Get out your favorite cast-iron skillet for the tastiest dinners. Cast iron provides even heat distribution for speedy cooking.

- Keep your kitchen shears handy. You'll find yourself using them again & again for snipping fresh herbs, chopping tomatoes right in the can and snipping the ends off fresh green beans.

- Fill the sink with hot soapy water when you start dinner, and just toss in pans and utensils as they're used. Clean-up will be a breeze!

Sweet & Tangy Fruit Dip, Page 24

CHAPTER ONE

Quick-to-Fix Appetizers & Snacks

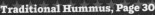

Traditional Hummus, Page 30

Bacon-Wrapped Pineapple Bites, Page 10

Bonnie Waters, Bloomington, IN

Cranberry-Jalapeño Salsa

This salsa has been a family favorite at Thanksgiving and other gatherings for many years. I have to make two or three batches! We grow our own jalapeños and green onions, so when in season, it's fresh from our garden. This salsa is also delicious as a sauce over roast turkey or pork for a meal or sandwich.

Makes 8 servings

14-oz. can whole-berry
  cranberry sauce
1 jalapeño pepper, halved, seeded
  and diced
1/4 c. fresh cilantro, snipped
2 green onions, sliced
1 t. lime juice
1/4 t. ground cumin
tortilla chips

In a bowl, combine all ingredients except tortilla chips. Stir until well blended. Serve at room temperature or cover and chill. Serve with tortilla chips.

Danyel Martin, Madisonville, KY

Crabmeat Dip

This recipe was given to me by my mom. It is wonderful to take to a potluck for work or a family gathering. I took this to a black-tie event with my husband's boss and it was the hit of the party.

Makes 20 servings

8-oz. pkg. light cream cheese,
  softened
1 t. lemon juice
2 t. onion, minced
1-1/2 T. crumbled blue cheese
12-oz. jar cocktail sauce
6-oz. can crabmeat, drained
assorted crackers

Blend together cream cheese, lemon juice, minced onion and blue cheese. Spread evenly on a plate; spread with cocktail sauce to cover. Sprinkle with crabmeat. Serve with crackers.

★ TASTY TIP ★ For a quick & tasty appetizer, spread toasted baguette slices with cream cheese and top with a dollop of cranberry salsa.

Cranberry-Jalapeño Salsa

Jessica Kraus, Delaware, OH

Bacon-Wrapped Pineapple Bites

These are so irresistible...the mixture of salty and sweet is amazing! You should probably double the recipe, because they'll go quickly.

Makes 10 servings

1 c. brown sugar, packed
16-oz. pkg. bacon, slices cut in half
20-oz. can pineapple chunks, drained
wooden toothpicks, soaked in water

Place brown sugar in a shallow bowl. Dredge each half-slice of bacon in brown sugar. Place one pineapple chunk on one end of each bacon piece and roll up; secure with a toothpick. Sprinkle rolls with remaining brown sugar. Arrange on a greased rack placed on a baking sheet. Bake at 375 degrees for 25 minutes, or until bacon is crisp.

★ FRUIT FACTS ★ How can you tell when a pineapple is ripe? Just check the base...if it's green, it's not ripe yet. If it's orange or mushy, it's too ripe. But if it's yellow and bright, it's just right.

Bacon-Wrapped Pineapple Bites

Andrea Durante, Hopedale, MA

Southwestern Smothered Potato Chips

I put this recipe together for a game-day party...it was quite a hit!

Serves 4 to 6

6 potatoes, sliced lengthwise
   1/8-inch thick
1/2 t. salt
2 T. olive oil
1/2 c. red onion, chopped
1 c. shredded Monterey Jack cheese
1 c. guacamole
1 c. salsa

Arrange potato slices in a single layer on a lightly greased baking sheet. Sprinkle with salt; drizzle with oil. Broil under low heat for about 10 minutes, until crisp but not burnt, checking often. Remove from oven. Sprinkle chips evenly with onion and cheese. Bake at 350 degrees for 5 minutes, until cheese is melted. To serve, top with small dollops of guacamole and salsa.

Marian Smith, Columbus, OH

Fiesta Guacamole

This was a tasty and welcome addition to our office Fiesta Party!

Makes 10 servings

4 avocados, peeled, pitted, cubed and
   mashed
2 tomatoes, diced
1/2 onion, diced
1 bunch fresh cilantro, chopped
1 jalapeño pepper, chopped
1 T. garlic, minced
juice of 2 limes

Blend together avocados and tomatoes. Stir in onion, cilantro, jalapeño and garlic. Add lime juice; mix well. Cover and refrigerate for 45 minutes before serving.

★ SPICY SECRET ★ **Make Southwestern Smothered Potato Chips with a little more kick...sprinkle with Cajun or barbecue seasoning!**

Southwestern Smothered Potato Chips

Paulette Alexander, Newfoundland, Canada

Chickpea & Red Pepper Dip

The first time I made this flavorful recipe, I knew it was a keeper... everybody loved it! Serve with toasted pita wedges.

Makes 8 servings, or about 2 cups

19-oz. can garbanzo beans, drained and rinsed
12-oz. jar roasted red peppers, drained and sliced
1/2 c. sour cream
1 to 2 cloves garlic, chopped
1/2 t. red pepper flakes
1/4 t. salt
1/4 t. pepper

Combine all ingredients in a food processor or blender. Process until smooth; transfer to a serving dish.

★ SAVVY SWAP ★ Try Chickpea & Red Pepper Dip as a healthy spread on sandwiches instead of mayonnaise. Serve on broiled fish, chicken or even to top baked potatoes instead of sour cream.

Patti Bogetti, Magnolia, DE

Patti's Pepper Poppers

This is my most requested party appetizer...they're irresistible! The longer you bake them, the milder they become.

Makes about 3-1/2 dozen

8-oz. pkg. cream cheese, softened
8-oz. pkg. shredded Cheddar Jack cheese
2 T. bacon bits
1/2 t. garlic salt
1/4 t. chili powder
20 jalapeño peppers, halved and seeded
1/2 c. Italian-seasoned dry bread crumbs

In a large bowl, blend cheeses, bacon bits and seasonings. Spoon one to 2 teaspoons of mixture into each pepper half; sprinkle with bread crumbs. Place on an ungreased 15"x10" jelly-roll pan. Bake, uncovered, at 300 degrees for 25 to 30 minutes.

Chickpea & Red Pepper Dip

Wendy Wright, New London, WI

Pepperoni Egg Rolls

My mother made these for our family's annual football party and they were such a hit...really different and tasty! Set out a bowl of warmed pizza sauce for dipping.

Makes one dozen

16-oz. pkg. egg roll wrappers
1 doz. pieces string cheese
8-oz. can pizza sauce
8-oz. pkg. sliced pepperoni
oil for deep frying

Lay out egg roll wrappers on a counter. Top each wrapper with a piece of string cheese, 2 tablespoons pizza sauce and 4 pepperoni slices. Roll up, tucking in the sides as you roll. In a deep fryer over high heat, heat several inches oil to 375 degrees. Add egg rolls, a few at a time. Cook for 2 to 3 minutes, or until golden. Remove with a slotted spoon. Drain on paper towels; let cool before serving.

Diane Cohen, The Woodlands, TX

Pizza Roll Snacks

Who needs frozen pizza rolls when it's a snap to make these yummy rolls? My girls love them for after-school snacks. If there are any leftovers, they warm up great in the microwave.

Makes 16

8-oz. tube refrigerated crescent rolls
3 T. pizza sauce
1/4 c. grated Parmesan cheese
16 slices pepperoni, divided
1/3 c. shredded mozzarella cheese, divided
Garnish: small fresh basil leaves

Unroll crescent roll dough but do not separate; press perforations to seal. Spread pizza sauce evenly over dough, leaving a one-inch border. Sprinkle with Parmesan cheese and roll up, starting with the long side. Using a sharp knife, cut roll into 16 slices. Place slices cut-side down on a greased baking sheet. Top each slice with one pepperoni slice and one teaspoon mozzarella cheese. Bake at 375 degrees for 9 to 11 minutes, until edges are golden and cheese melts. Garnish with basil leaves..

Pepperoni Egg Rolls

Anita Williams, Pikeville, KY

Fresh Fruit Kabobs & Poppy Seed Dip

Try grilling these kabobs for a new spin. Place skewers over medium-high heat for 3 to 5 minutes...yum!

Serves 8 to 10

6 c. fresh fruit like strawberries, kiwi, pineapple, honeydew and cantaloupe, peeled and cut into bite-size cubes or slices
8 to 10 wooden skewers

Arrange fruit pieces alternately on skewers. Serve Poppy Seed Dip alongside fruit kabobs.

Poppy Seed Dip:

1 c. vanilla yogurt
2 T. honey
4 t. lime juice
1 t. vanilla extract
1 t. poppy seed

Stir together ingredients in a small bowl. Keep chilled.

★ DOUBLE DUTY ★ Serve these fresh fruit kabobs as a healthy breakfast side! They can even be slipped into breakfast smoothies or frosty glasses of juice.

Fresh Fruit Kabobs & Poppy Seed Dip

Anne Alesauskas, Minocqua, WI

Avocado Feta Dip

My family doesn't care for tomatoes but we love red peppers...so we love this!

Makes 3 cups, serves 12

2 avocados, halved, pitted and diced
3/4 c. crumbled feta cheese
1 red pepper, diced
1 green onion, thinly sliced
1 T. lemon juice
2 t. dill weed
1/4 t. salt
1/4 t. pepper

Combine all ingredients in a serving bowl; mix until well blended.

Chris Nelson, New Berlin, WI

Quick & Easy Summer Salsa

There is absolutely nothing like garden-fresh salsa. If you can't wait for it to chill, no problem...it's terrific enjoyed right away!

Makes 2-1/2 to 3 cups, serves 6

10 roma tomatoes, chopped
1 c. fresh cilantro, chopped
1/2 c. red onion, chopped
1 T. vinegar
1/2 c. olive oil
juice of 2 key limes
tortilla chips

Combine all ingredients except chips in a bowl; stir to blend. Refrigerate until chilled. Serve with tortilla chips.

★ DIPPING DELIGHT ★ **A tray of colorful vegetables for your next family get-together...red, orange and green pepper strips, radish roses, broccoli flowerets, green onions, cherry tomatoes, celery sticks, pea pods and of course, Avocado Feta Dip!**

Avocado Feta Dip

Lisanne Miller, Canton, MS

Sun-Dried Tomato Toasties

These are so quick to make and are so pretty to serve. I serve them on a wood serving tray while they are still warm.

Makes 2 to 3 dozen

1/2 c. sun-dried tomato and olive relish
2-1/4 oz. can chopped black olives, drained
2 t. garlic, chopped
8-oz. pkg. shredded mozzarella cheese, divided
1 loaf French bread, thinly sliced

Mix together relish, olives, garlic and 1/4 cup cheese; spread evenly on bread slices. Arrange bread on an ungreased baking sheet; sprinkle the bread pieces with remaining cheese. Bake at 300 degrees for 4 to 5 minutes, until cheese melts; serve immediately.

Judy Olson, Alberta, Canada

Hot Mushroom Dip

I make this delicious dip often when people come to visit...it always gets eaten up quickly! Good with crackers, fresh veggies and even cubes of bread.

Makes about 1-1/2 cups

2-1/2 c. mushrooms, chopped
1/2 c. green onions, chopped
1/4 c. margarine
2 T. all-purpose flour
1/2 t. paprika
1/4 c. milk
1 c. sour cream, divided
1/2 t. salt
1/2 t. pepper
1/8 t. cayenne pepper
assorted crackers

In a skillet over medium heat, sauté mushrooms and onions in margarine until nearly tender. Stir in flour and paprika; add milk and 1/2 cup sour cream. Cook over low heat until mushrooms are tender. Stir in remaining sour cream and seasonings. Serve hot with crackers.

★ TASTY TWIST ★ Serve your favorite dip with a twist! Just spread dip onto flour tortillas, roll up jelly-roll style and cut into one-inch slices. Try using colorful flavored wraps like sun-dried tomato & basil, garlic-herb or chipotle chile...top each with a slice of olive or jalapeño pepper.

Sun-Dried Tomato Toasties

Jill Ball, Highland, UT

Sweet & Tangy Fruit Dip

As a mother, I'm always looking for easy, healthy snack ideas, so I created this recipe.

Makes 10 servings

1 c. low-fat cottage cheese
3 T. low-fat plain yogurt
2 t. honey
1 T. orange juice
2-1/2 T. orange marmalade
2 T. unsweetened flaked coconut
favorite fresh fruit, sliced

Place all ingredients except coconut and fruit in a food processor. Process until smooth and creamy. Stir in coconut. Refrigerate until chilled. Serve with a variety of fresh fruit.

Lisa Blumberg, Knoxville, TN

Lemony-Fresh Dill Dip

Enjoy this refreshing dip like we do... by dunking blanched fresh green beans in it. Yummy!

Makes 4 servings, or 1-1/3 cups

1 c. plain low-fat yogurt
1/3 c. fresh dill, chopped
1 t. lemon zest
1 T. lemon juice
salt and pepper to taste

Combine all ingredients in a bowl; stir well. Cover and chill before serving.

★ FRESH TIP ★ Set up a fruit salad bar on the kitchen counter and add some fun to mealtime or snacktime. Bowls of fresh strawberries, blueberries, grapes, kiwi, sliced apples and bananas along with some Sweet & Tangy Fruit Dip are all yummy choices.

Sweet & Tangy Fruit Dip

Jo Ann, Gooseberry Patch

Apple & Brie Toasts

These little tidbits of flavor are so showy and easy to make. We enjoy them often!

Makes 2-1/2 dozen

1 baguette, cut into 1/4-inch-thick slices
1/4 c. brown sugar, packed
1/4 c. chopped walnuts
3 T. butter, melted
13.2-oz. pkg. Brie cheese, thinly sliced
3 Granny Smith apples and/or Braeburn apples, cored and sliced

Arrange baguette slices on an ungreased baking sheet; bake at 350 degrees until lightly toasted. Set aside. Mix together brown sugar, walnuts and butter. Top each slice of bread with a cheese slice, an apple slice and 1/2 teaspoon of brown sugar mixture. Bake at 350 degrees until cheese melts, 2 to 4 minutes.

Cindy Snyder, Kittanning, PA

Cheddar Apple Pie Dip

This is a great appetizer for a fall gathering of friends around a toasty fire. I also like to serve it at family gatherings. I serve it with whole-grain crackers or small pieces of toasted whole-grain bread.

Makes 8 servings

1/4 c. brown sugar, packed
1/4 t. cinnamon
1 red apple, cored and finely chopped
1 Granny Smith apple, cored and finely chopped
1/2 c. pecan pieces, coarsely chopped
8-oz. pkg. light cream cheese, softened
1-1/2 c. reduced-fat shredded sharp Cheddar cheese
1/4 c. light sour cream

Combine brown sugar and cinnamon in a bowl; stir in apples and pecans. Mix cream cheese and Cheddar cheese; add sour cream, stirring well to blend. Spread mixture in a 9" pie plate; top with apple mixture. Bake, uncovered, at 375 degrees for 20 minutes, or until heated through.

★ EASY CHEESY ★ For an easy yet elegant appetizer, try a cheese platter. Choose a soft cheese, a hard cheese and a semi-soft or crumbly cheese. Add a basket of crisp crackers, crusty baguette slices and some sliced apples or pears. So simple, yet sure to please guests!

Apple & Brie Toasts

Sandi Giverson, Vero Beach, FL

Marianne's Cranberry Roll-Ups

One of the girls I work with, Marianne Hudgins, always has the best recipes! With her permission, here is one of my favorites.

Makes 10 servings

8-oz. container light whipped cream cheese
8-oz. pkg. crumbled feta cheese
6-oz. pkg. dried cranberries
3 T. chives, chopped
4 10-inch whole-grain flour tortillas

Combine all ingredients except tortillas together; blend until smooth. Spread mixture over tortillas, roll up and wrap in plastic wrap; chill until ready to serve. Cut each roll into one-inch slices.

Lynda McCormick, Burkburnett, TX

Greek Pita Pizza

These pizzas are so deep and rich in color and they are very nutritious as well.

Makes 8 servings

10-oz. pkg. frozen chopped spinach, thawed and well drained
4 green onions, chopped
1 T. fresh dill, chopped
garlic salt and pepper to taste
4 whole-wheat pita rounds, split
4 roma tomatoes, sliced 1/2-inch thick
1/2 c. crumbled feta cheese with basil & tomato
dried oregano or Greek seasoning to taste

Mix spinach, onions and dill in a small bowl. Season with garlic salt and pepper; set aside. Place pita rounds on ungreased baking sheets. Arrange tomato slices among pitas. Spread spinach mixture evenly over tomatoes; spread cheese over tomatoes. Sprinkle with desired seasoning. Bake at 450 degrees for 10 to 15 minutes, until crisp. Cut into wedges.

Marianne's Cranberry Roll-Ups

Louise McGaha, Clinton, TN

Traditional Hummus

I love this recipe...it's just right for a snack or a quick appetizer.

Makes 2 cups, serves 10

2 15-oz. cans garbanzo beans, drained and rinsed
1/2 c. warm water
3 T. lime or lemon juice
1 T. tahini sesame seed paste
1-1/2 t. ground cumin
1 T. garlic, minced
1/4 t. salt

Place all ingredients in a food processor or blender. Process until mixture is very smooth, about 4 minutes. If a thinner consistency is desired, add an extra tablespoon or 2 of water. Transfer to a serving bowl.

Trudy Williams, Middlesex, NC

Nacho Chicken Dip

We love this delicious dip at parties... it's even good as a meal, paired with a side salad.

Makes 2 cups, serves 10

16-oz. can refried beans
12-oz. can chicken, drained and flaked
16-oz. jar chunky salsa
8-oz. pkg. shredded Mexican-blend cheese
tortilla chips

Layer beans, chicken, salsa and cheese in a lightly greased one-quart casserole dish. Bake, uncovered, at 350 degrees for 30 minutes, or until cheese is bubbly. Serve hot with tortilla chips.

Traditional Hummus

Jane Kirsch, Weymouth, MA

Feta Squares

These tasty little goodies are so easy to make and go fast!

Serves 8 to 10

8-oz container crumbled feta cheese
8-oz. pkg. cream cheese, softened
2 T. olive oil
3 cloves garlic, finely chopped
1 loaf sliced party pumpernickel
   bread
1 pt. grape tomatoes, halved
2 to 3 T. fresh chives, finely chopped

In a bowl, mix feta cheese, cream cheese, olive oil and garlic. Spread mixture on pumpernickel bread slices. Place on ungreased baking sheets. Top each square with a tomato half; sprinkle with chives. Bake at 350 degrees for 15 minutes.

★ GO GREEK ★ Give garlic bread a Greek twist...brush bread slices with olive oil, sprinkle with lemon-pepper, oregano and garlic. Top with feta cheese and sliced Kalamata olives. Delicious!

Mary Bettuchy, Columbia, SC

Smoked Pimento Cheese Dip

We're a military family, so we've been stationed all over the country and get to try different regional foods. Here in South Carolina, one of the most delicious things I've discovered is pimento cheese! The smoky flavor is my own spin on this classic.

Makes 8 servings

8-oz. pkg. smoked Cheddar cheese,
   shredded
8-oz. pkg. cream cheese, softened
2 4-oz. jars pimentos or roasted red
   peppers, drained and diced
1/4 c. mayonnaise
1/2 t. smoked salt or 1/4 t. smoke-
   flavored cooking sauce
1/4 t. hot pepper sauce
1/4 t. red pepper flakes
pita chips

In a food processor or blender, combine all ingredients except pita chips. Pulse until combined. If mixture is too thick, add a little more mayonnaise. If more smoky flavor or heat is desired, add more smoke or hot sauce to taste. Serve with pita chips.

Feta Squares

Ann Farris, Biscoe, AZ

Prosciutto-Wrapped Asparagus

This simple and pretty presentation of asparagus is always a hit at any party or event.

Makes 6 servings

1 bunch asparagus, about 10 pieces, trimmed
1 T. olive oil
1 t. kosher salt
1 t. pepper
3-oz. pkg. sliced prosciutto, cut into strips with fat removed
Optional: lemon slices

Toss asparagus with oil, salt and pepper. Arrange in a single layer on an ungreased rimmed baking sheet. Bake at 400 degrees for 5 minutes. Allow to cool slightly. Wrap each asparagus spear with a strip of prosciutto. Return to oven and bake for 4 more minutes or until asparagus is crisp-tender and prosciutto is slightly browned. Serve warm or at room temperature, garnished with thin lemon slices, if desired.

Paulette Walters, Newfoundland, Canada

Curry Chicken Party Rolls

I love being able to make this tasty appetizer with ingredients I already have on hand. It makes a lot of servings and takes no time at all! You can even use raisins or apples instead of grapes.

Serves 8 to 10

1 boneless, skinless chicken breast, cooked and shredded
3 to 4 T. mayonnaise
2 to 3 T. grapes, thinly sliced
2 T. celery, finely diced
curry powder to taste
3 soft sandwich wraps

In a bowl, mix chicken with just enough mayonnaise to hold together. Add grapes, celery and curry powder. Spread mixture on wraps and roll up; cut into one-inch lengths. Serve immediately, or cover and refrigerate until serving time.

★ QUICK TIP ★ Quick & easy appetizers... wrap pear slices or melon wedges with prosciutto or thinly sliced turkey...yum!

Prosciutto-Wrapped Asparagus

Diane Stevenson, Marion, IA

Yummy Snack Mix

A wonderful blend of flavors and textures makes this snack mix a great addition to any party.

Serves 20

2 c. bite-size crispy corn cereal
2 c. bite-size crispy rice cereal
2 c. round corn cereal
1/2 c. whole cashews
1/2 c. whole almonds
1/2 c. raisins
1/2 c. dried apricots, chopped

1/2 c. butter, melted
1/2 c. sugar
1 t. cinnamon

In a large bowl, combine cereals, cashews, almonds, raisins and apricots. Pour melted butter over mixture and toss lightly. In a separate bowl, mix together sugar and cinnamon; sprinkle over cereal mixture. Mix well. Pour into a large shallow baking pan. Bake at 250 degrees for one hour, stirring every 15 minutes. Cool.

★ KID-FRIENDLY ★ Remember the fun of digging down in a box of caramel corn and peanuts for the little prize? Make some homemade snack mix and pack it up in individual Chinese take-out cartons, wrap little toys and treasures in wax paper and hide 'em in the cartons for "remember when" giggles!

Yummy Snack Mix

Carole Larkins, Elmendorf Air Force Base, AK

Artichoke-Garlic Dip

Serve this savory spread in a hollowed-out sourdough bread loaf, with chunks of bread and hearty crackers for dipping.

Makes about 3-1/2 cups

14-oz. can artichokes, drained and chopped
1/2 c. grated Parmesan cheese
8-oz. pkg. cream cheese, softened
1/2 c. mayonnaise
2 cloves garlic, minced
1/2 t. dill weed
Optional: additional Parmesan cheese

Combine artichokes, cheeses, mayonnaise, garlic and dill weed in an ungreased 10" pie plate. If desired, sprinkle with additional Parmesan cheese. Bake, uncovered, at 400 degrees for 15 minutes, or until golden.

Jo Ann, Gooseberry Patch

Pecan-Stuffed Deviled Eggs

Make these deviled eggs fun and festive by adding snipped parsley and chopped pecans as a garnish.

Makes 6 servings

6 eggs, hard-boiled and peeled
1/4 c. mayonnaise
1 t. onion, grated
1/2 t. fresh parsley, chopped
1/2 t. dry mustard
1/8 t. salt
1/3 c. pecans, coarsely chopped
Garnish: fresh parsley, chopped pecans

Cut eggs in half lengthwise and carefully remove yolks. Mash yolks in a small bowl. Stir in mayonnaise and next 4 ingredients; blend well. Stir in pecans. Spoon or pipe yolk mixture evenly into egg-white halves. Garnish, as desired.

Artichoke-Garlic Dip

Donna Cannon, Tulsa, OK

Roasted Red Pepper Spread

For years, my large Italian family would come together at one of our homes for Christmas Eve or post-Christmas get-togethers. We each signed up to bring appetizers, main dishes, side dishes, desserts and beverages. This delicious spread was always a favorite.

Makes 2 to 3 cups

8-oz. container mayonnaise
8-oz. container sour cream
7-oz. jar roasted red peppers, drained and liquid reserved
1 handful fresh basil, loosely packed
salt and pepper to taste
Melba toast rounds, snack crackers, vegetable slices

In a food processor, combine mayonnaise and sour cream. Add peppers, basil, salt and pepper; pulse until well-combined. Blend in reserved liquid, one tablespoon at a time, to desired consistency. Spoon into a serving dish or bread bowl. Serve with Melba toast, crackers or vegetables.

Cynde Sonnier, Mont Belvieu, TX

Pineapple-Pecan Cheese Spread

This is a delicious, fast-fix recipe and always yummy with fresh veggies or pieces of toasted whole-grain bread. The combination of the sweet crushed pineapple and the spicy chiles and red peppers is just perfect!

Makes 8 servings

2 8-oz. pkgs. light cream cheese, softened
1-1/2 c. reduced-fat shredded Cheddar cheese
3/4 c. chopped pecans, toasted and divided
3/4 c. crushed pineapple, drained
4-oz. can chopped green chiles, drained
2 T. roasted red peppers, chopped
1/2 t. garlic powder

In a large bowl, beat cream cheese until smooth. Add Cheddar cheese, 3/4 cup pecans, pineapple, chiles, red pepper and garlic powder; beat until thoroughly combined. Transfer to a serving dish. Cover and refrigerate. When ready to serve, sprinkle with remaining pecans.

Roasted Red Pepper Spread

Celestina Torrez, Camden, NJ

Mini Ham & Swiss Frittatas

I first started making these for my toddlers as easy-to-handle mini omelets. My husband thought they would be yummy as appetizers too, so now I serve them when we're watching the big game on TV, or for a simple appetizer when we are having a fresh salad. They're still a hit with my kids too!

Makes 2 dozen

8-oz. pkg. cooked ham, diced
2/3 c. shredded Swiss cheese
1/4 c. fresh chives, chopped
pepper to taste
8 eggs, beaten

In a bowl, mix together ham, cheese, chives and pepper; set aside. Spray a 13"x9" baking pan with non-stick vegetable spray. Sprinkle cheese mixture evenly over pan. Pour eggs evenly over top of cheese mixture. Bake at 375 degrees until golden, about 13 minutes. Serve warm.

Marcia Marcoux, Charlton, MA

Pepperoni Puffs

These tasty morsels are really easy to stir up and hard to resist...you might want to make a double batch!

Makes 2 dozen

1 c. all-purpose flour
1 t. baking powder
1 c. milk
1 egg, beaten
1 c. shredded Cheddar cheese
1-1/2 c. pepperoni, diced
Garnish: warmed pizza sauce

Combine flour, baking powder, milk, egg and cheese in a bowl; mix well. Stir in pepperoni; let stand for 15 minutes. Spoon into greased mini muffin cups, filling 3/4 full. Bake at 350 degrees for 25 to 35 minutes, until golden. Serve with warmed pizza sauce for dipping.

★ IN A PINCH ★ **Whip up some no-cooking-needed pizza sauce in a jiffy. In a blender, combine a can of seasoned diced tomatoes, a little garlic and a shake of Italian seasoning. Purée to the desired consistency.**

Mini Ham & Swiss Frittatas

Egg & Bacon Quesadillas, Page 58

CHAPTER TWO

Easy Sunrise Breakfasts

Scrambled Egg Wrap, Page 52

Yummy Blueberry Waffles, Page 48

Donna Jones, Mikado, MI

Spicy Black Bean Scrambled Eggs

One day, I was tired of my usual breakfast choices. I had lots of my mother-in-law's homemade salsa on hand and some leftover black beans in the fridge. Added to typically boring scrambled eggs, the result was a dish I couldn't get enough of. Try it, you'll like it too!

Makes one serving

1/4 c. canned black beans, drained and rinsed
1/4 c. chunky salsa
1/8 t. chili powder
Optional: 1/8 t. red pepper flakes
2 eggs, beaten
6-inch corn tortilla

1/4 c. shredded sharp Cheddar cheese
Optional: additional salsa

Spray a small skillet with non-stick vegetable spray. Over medium heat, cook beans, salsa and desired seasonings for one minute, stirring frequently. Add eggs; stir to combine. Continue cooking and stirring until eggs are fully cooked. Place tortilla on a microwave-safe dinner plate and microwave for 10 seconds, until warmed. Spoon egg mixture onto tortilla. Top with cheese and more salsa, if desired. Serve immediately.

★ FLAVOR BURST ★ Add frozen mixed veggies to scrambled eggs, chicken noodle soup or even mac & cheese for a meal with a veggie punch!

Spicy Black Bean Scrambled Eggs

Jennifer Bontrager, Oklahoma City, OK

Yummy Blueberry Waffles

When I was a little girl, my grandpa owned a blueberry farm. The berries were so delicious that we always took home several gallons when our summer visit was over. This waffle recipe cooks up nice and fluffy...and the farm-fresh blueberries only make them better!

Makes 4 waffles

2 eggs
2 c. all-purpose flour
1-3/4 c. milk
1/2 c. oil
1 T. sugar
4 t. baking powder
1/4 t. salt
1/2 t. vanilla extract
1 to 1-1/2 c. blueberries

In a large bowl, beat eggs with an electric mixer on medium speed until fluffy. Add remaining ingredients except berries; beat just until smooth. Spray a waffle iron with non-stick vegetable spray. Pour batter by 1/2 cupfuls onto the preheated waffle iron. Scatter desired amount of berries over batter. Bake according to manufacturer's directions, until golden.

Jen Thomas, Santa Rosa, CA

French Toast Pick-Up Sticks

Our kids love this French toast they can eat with their hands! Save time by making ahead and freezing. Pop in the toaster to serve.

Makes 2 to 4 servings

2 eggs, beaten
3/4 c. milk
1 t. vanilla extract
4 slices bread, each cut into 4 strips
1 T. butter
Garnish: maple syrup, favorite preserves

Whisk together eggs, milk and vanilla in a shallow bowl. Dip bread strips, soaking well. Melt butter in a skillet over medium heat. Add bread strips; cook until golden on both sides. Serve warm with syrup or preserves for dipping.

Yummy Blueberry Waffles

Janice Barr, Lincoln, NE

Savory Egg Bake

My late husband always told me how much he liked this simple egg dish. He asked for it often...I think you'll enjoy it too!

Makes 2 servings

3 eggs, beaten
1/4 c. sour cream
1/4 t. salt
1 tomato, chopped
1 green onion, sliced
1/4 c. shredded Cheddar cheese

In a small bowl, beat eggs, sour cream and salt together. Stir in tomato, onion and cheese. Pour into a greased 2-cup casserole dish or ramekin. Bake, uncovered, at 350 degrees for 25 to 30 minutes, until a knife tip inserted in center tests clean.

Courtney Stultz, Columbus, KS

Veggie Egg Muffins

As a busy mom, mornings are crazy for me. I love finding shortcuts anywhere I can and these healthy muffins are perfect. They are loaded with veggies for great nutrition. They freeze well too!

Makes 20 muffins

18 eggs or egg white equivalent, beaten
6-oz. container plain yogurt or 3/4 c. milk
1 t. dried sage
1 t. sea salt
1/2 t. pepper
1 c. broccoli, finely chopped
1/2 c. cauliflower, finely chopped
1/2 c. carrots, peeled and finely chopped
1 to 2 c. shredded Cheddar cheese
Garnish: sour cream, salsa, catsup or sriracha sauce

Combine all ingredients except garnish in a large bowl; whisk until blended. Pour into 20 ungreased muffin cups, filling 2/3 full. Bake at 375 degrees for about 20 to 25 minutes, until eggs are set and golden. Garnish as desired. To freeze, let muffins cool completely. Store in a plastic freezer bag or container for up to 3 months. Reheat in microwave or oven.

Savory Egg Bake

Joyceann Dreibelbis, Wooster, OH

Scrambled Egg Wrap

You'll never be tempted to skip breakfast again after trying this tasty breakfast treat! It takes just 10 minutes to make one serving and is so easy to double or triple. Enjoy!

Makes one serving

2 eggs, lightly beaten
1 whole-wheat flour tortilla
2 T. herb-flavored cream cheese, softened
2 T. shredded Cheddar cheese
1-1/2 t. fresh basil, chopped
1-1/2 t. fresh chives, chopped
1 T. salsa

Coat a small skillet with non-stick vegetable spray; heat over medium-low heat. Add eggs and cook for 2 minutes, stirring constantly. Spread tortilla with cream cheese; top with eggs and remaining ingredients. Roll up tortilla, folding in sides; place on an ungreased baking sheet. Bake at 300 degrees for 3 minutes, or until warmed through.

Karen McCann, Marion, OH

Justin's Skillet Breakfast

Sausage, hashbrowns, chiles and cheese...there's no boring breakfast here!

Makes 6 servings

1/2 lb. ground pork sausage
2 c. frozen shredded hashbrowns
10-oz. can diced tomatoes with green chiles, drained
8-oz. pkg. pasteurized process cheese spread, diced
6 eggs, beaten
2 T. water

Brown sausage in a large cast-iron skillet over medium heat; drain. Add hashbrowns and tomatoes. Cook for 5 minutes; sprinkle with cheese. Beat eggs with water; pour evenly into skillet. Reduce heat to low; cover and cook for 10 to 12 minutes, until eggs are set in center and cheese is melted. Uncover; let stand 5 minutes before cutting into wedges.

Scrambled Egg Wrap

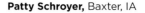

Kathrine Moore, British Columbia, Canada

Kathy's Denver Sandwich

This is our idea of a good breakfast sandwich! Try it with diced ham too.

Makes 3 sandwiches

4 slices bacon, chopped
1 T. onion, chopped
2 T. green pepper, chopped
3 eggs, beaten
1/4 c. shredded Cheddar cheese
6 slices bread, toasted and buttered

In a skillet over medium heat, cook bacon until partially done but not crisp. Add onion and green pepper; cook until softened. Add eggs and cook to desired doneness. Sprinkle with cheese; cover and let stand until melted. Cut into 3 pieces; serve each between 2 slices of toast.

Patty Schroyer, Baxter, IA

Zesty Brunch Quiche

Try using peach or apricot salsa for a whole new taste.

Makes 6 servings

1 c. shredded Cheddar cheese
4 slices bacon, crisply cooked and crumbled
2 green onions, thinly sliced
9-inch frozen pie crust
3 eggs, beaten
1/2 c. milk
1/2 c. salsa

Sprinkle cheese, bacon and onions into pie crust; set aside. Whisk eggs, milk and salsa together; pour into pie crust. Carefully place on a baking sheet; bake at 375 degrees for 35 minutes. Let stand 10 minutes before slicing.

★ QUICK FIX ★ Bake a family-favorite omelet or quiche in muffin cups for individual servings in a jiffy. When making minis, reduce the baking time by about 10 minutes, and test for doneness with a toothpick.

Kathy's Denver Sandwich

Tina Butler, Royse City, TX

Green Monster Smoothie

Wanting my children to eat healthier, I tried these yummy smoothies filled with bananas, almond milk and spinach. They were a big hit...the kids couldn't even tell spinach is added!

Serves 3 to 4

1 c. vanilla almond milk
1 to 2 bananas, sliced and frozen
1 c. fresh or frozen spinach
1/2 c. ice
Optional: 1 T. honey

Combine milk, bananas, spinach and ice in a blender; process on high setting until smooth. Add honey if a sweeter taste is desired. Pour into glasses to serve.

Michelle Case, Yardley, PA

Break-of-Day Berry Parfait

So pretty served in a parfait or champagne glass!

Makes 2 servings

1 c. strawberries, hulled and
   sliced
1/2 c. raspberries
1/4 c. blackberries
1 c. bran & raisin cereal
6-oz. container strawberry
   yogurt

In a bowl, combine berries; divide into 2 small bowls. Top each with cereal. Spoon yogurt over top.

★ MAKE AHEAD ★ Are breakfast smoothies a favorite at your house? Mix them up the night before, then pour into canning jars and tuck in the fridge. Perfect portions, ready to shake and go!

Green Monster Smoothie

Joshua Logan, Corpus Christi, TX

Egg & Bacon Quesadillas

So quick and so yummy...they will ask for more.

Makes 4 servings

2 T. butter, divided
4 8-inch flour tortillas
5 eggs, beaten
1/2 c. milk
2 8-oz. pkgs. shredded Cheddar
  cheese
6 to 8 slices bacon, crisply cooked
  and crumbled
Optional: salsa, sour cream

Lightly spread about 1/4 teaspoon butter on one side of each tortilla; set aside. In a bowl, beat eggs and milk until combined. Pour egg mixture into a hot, lightly greased skillet; cook and stir over medium heat until done. Remove scrambled eggs to a dish and keep warm. Melt remaining butter in the skillet and add a tortilla, buttered-side down. Layer with 1/4 of the cheese, 1/2 of the eggs and 1/2 of the bacon. Top with 1/4 of the cheese and a tortilla, buttered-side up. Cook one to 2 minutes on each side, until golden. Repeat with remaining ingredients. Cut each into 4 wedges and serve with salsa and sour cream, if desired.

★ ALL HANDS ON DECK ★ Have an all-finger-food breakfast. Serve wedges of Egg & Bacon Quesadillas alongside fresh carrot and celery dippers with cups of creamy salad dressing. For dessert, chocolate fondue!

Egg & Bacon Quesadillas

SUNRISE BREAKFASTS

Tonya Sheppard, Galveston, TX

Huevos Rancheros to Go-Go

Serve these eggs with sliced fresh avocado for a deliciously different breakfast.

Makes 4 servings

2 c. red or green tomatillo salsa
4 eggs
4 8-inch corn tortillas
1-1/2 c. shredded Monterey Jack cheese or crumbled queso fresco

Lightly grease a cast-iron skillet; place over medium heat. Pour salsa into skillet; bring to a simmer. With a spoon, make 4 wells in salsa. Crack an egg into each well, taking care not to break the yolks. Reduce heat to low; cover and poach eggs for 3 minutes. Remove skillet from heat and top with eggs. Transfer each egg and a scoop of salsa to a tortilla; roll up. Sprinkle with cheese.

Megan Brooks, Antioch, TN

Diner-Style Corned Beef Hash

Top each portion with an egg... sunny-side up, of course!

Makes 2 servings

1 T. oil
2 potatoes, peeled and diced
1 onion, chopped
12-oz. can corned beef, chopped
1 t. pepper
2-1/2 T. cider vinegar, divided

Heat oil in a skillet over medium-high heat. Add potatoes and onion; sauté until light golden. Stir in corned beef, pepper and one tablespoon vinegar. Cook for 3 to 5 minutes; stir in remaining vinegar. Partially cover skillet. Reduce heat and cook for about 20 minutes, stirring occasionally, until potatoes are tender.

Huevos Rancheros to Go-Go

Micki Stephens, Marion, OH

Rise & Shine Breakfast Pizza

You will enjoy tasting the layers of all your breakfast favorites in this dish!

Serves 8 to 10

2-lb. pkg. frozen shredded
   hashbrowns
1-1/2 c. shredded Cheddar cheese,
   divided
7 eggs, beaten
1/2 c. milk
salt and pepper to taste
10 to 12 pork breakfast sausage
   patties, cooked

Prepare hashbrowns according to package directions; spread on an ungreased baking sheet or pizza pan. Top with 1/2 cup cheese; set aside. Whisk together eggs and milk in a microwave-safe bowl; microwave on high 3 minutes, then scramble eggs well with a whisk. Return to microwave and cook 3 more minutes; whisk well to scramble. Layer eggs on top of cheese; add salt and pepper to taste. Top with remaining cheese. Arrange sausage patties on top. Bake at 400 degrees for 10 minutes, or until cheese is melted. Cut into squares or wedges to serve.

★ HOT TIP ★ If you're turning on the oven to bake Rise & Shine Breakfast Pizza, why not bake a whole oven full of potatoes while you're at it? Once cooked, you can grate or dice them for hashbrowns, soups or casseroles, slice them for home fries or whip up a quick potato salad!

Rise & Shine Breakfast Pizza

Julie Ann Perkins, Anderson, IN

Peanut Butter French Toast

Who can resist the classic taste of peanut butter & jelly?

Makes 2 servings

4 slices white or whole-wheat bread
1/2 c. creamy peanut butter
2 T. grape jelly
3 eggs, beaten
1/4 c. milk
2 T. butter
Garnish: powdered sugar

Use bread, peanut butter and jelly to make 2 sandwiches; set aside. In a bowl, whisk together eggs and milk. Dip each sandwich into egg mixture. Melt butter in a non-stick skillet over medium heat. Add sandwiches to skillet and cook until golden, about 2 to 3 minutes on each side. Sprinkle with powdered sugar; cut diagonally into triangles.

Recipe and Photo Courtesy of IowaEgg.org

PB & J Oatmeal

This classic oatmeal breakfast just became a show-stopper with the addition of peanut butter and strawberries.

Makes 4 servings

1 c. long-cooking oats, uncooked
2 c. unsweetened vanilla almond milk
4 egg whites, beaten
1/2 t. sugar
1/4 c. crunchy or creamy peanut butter
8 strawberries, hulled and sliced

In a medium saucepan, combine oats and almond milk. Cook over medium heat for 8 to 10 minutes or until all the liquid has been absorbed. Add egg whites to the oats and stir continuously, one to 2 minutes. (This will keep the egg whites from immediately scrambling.) Stir in sugar. Remove from heat and portion into bowls. Stir in peanut butter and top with strawberries.

Peanut Butter French Toast

Vickie, Gooseberry Patch

Fiesta Corn Tortilla Quiche

Use hot or mild sausage...the choice is up to you.

Makes 4 servings

1 lb. ground pork sausage
5 6-inch corn tortillas
4-oz. can chopped green chiles, drained
1 c. shredded Monterey Jack cheese
1 c. shredded Cheddar cheese
6 eggs, beaten
1/2 c. whipping cream
1/2 c. small-curd cottage cheese

Brown sausage in a cast-iron skillet over medium heat; drain. Set sausage aside; wipe skillet clean. Arrange tortillas in the same skillet, overlapping on the bottom and extending up the sides. Spoon sausage, chiles and cheeses into tortilla-lined skillet. In a bowl, beat together remaining ingredients. Pour egg mixture over sausage mixture. Transfer skillet to oven. Bake, uncovered, at 375 degrees for 45 minutes, or until golden. Cut into wedges to serve.

★ FREEZE IT ★ If you only use part of a package of tortillas, it's fine to freeze the leftover ones in an airtight container. For the best texture, let them thaw overnight in the fridge before using.

Fiesta Corn Tortilla Quiche

Angela Leikem, Silverton, OR

Good Morning Chile Relleno

Serve with fruit salad and sausage links for a spicy breakfast.

Serves 8 to 10

6-oz. pkg. shredded Cheddar cheese
16-oz. pkg. shredded Monterey
   Jack cheese
2 4-oz. cans chopped green chiles
4 eggs, beaten
1 c. evaporated milk
1/4 c. all-purpose flour
Garnish: cherry tomatoes, fresh
   parsley

Sprinkle cheeses and chiles together alternately in a greased 13"x9" baking pan. Whisk together eggs, milk and flour in a medium bowl and pour over cheese mixture. Bake, uncovered, at 350 degrees for 30 minutes. Let cool slightly before serving. Garnish as desired.

Sonya Labbe, Quebec, Canada

Ham & Gruyère Egg Cup

This recipe is always on our Sunday brunch table. It is quick, easy and tasty...very pretty too!

Makes one dozen

12 thin slices deli ham
3/4 c. shredded Gruyère cheese
1 doz. eggs
salt and pepper to taste
3/4 c. half-and-half
2 T. grated Parmesan cheese
Garnish: pepper

Spray 12 muffin cups or ramekins with non-stick vegetable spray. Line each muffin cup or ramekin with a slice of ham folded in half. Top each ham slice with one tablespoon Gruyère cheese, an egg cracked into the cup, a sprinkle of salt and pepper, one tablespoon half-and-half and 1/2 teaspoon Parmesan cheese. Place muffin tin or ramekins on a baking sheet. Bake at 450 degrees for 15 minutes, or until eggs are set. If using a muffin tin, allow baked eggs to cool several minutes before removing them from the muffin tin. Cool slightly before serving in ramekins. Sprinkle with pepper.

Good Morning Chile Relleno

Vickie, Gooseberry Patch

Black Bean Breakfast Bowls

We love to serve this dish for breakfast on weekends. It looks so special...and tastes so yummy!

Makes 2 servings

2 T. olive oil
4 eggs, beaten
15-1/2 oz. can black beans, drained and rinsed
1 avocado, peeled, pitted and sliced
1/4 c. shredded Cheddar cheese
1/4 c. favorite salsa
salt and pepper to taste

Heat oil in a skillet over medium heat. Add eggs and scramble as desired, 3 to 5 minutes; remove from heat. Place beans in a microwave-safe bowl. Microwave on high until warm, one to 2 minutes. To serve, divide into bowls; top each bowl with eggs, avocado, cheese and salsa. Season with salt and pepper.

★ WRAP IT ★ Any egg dish turns into a portable breakfast when spooned into a pita or rolled up in a tortilla!

Black Bean Breakfast Bowls

Nicole Millard, Mendon, MI

Grandma McKindley's Waffles

You can't go wrong with an old-fashioned waffle breakfast... the topping choices are endless!

Makes 8 to 10 waffles

2 c. all-purpose flour
1 T. baking powder
1/4 t. salt
2 eggs, separated
1-1/2 c. milk
3 T. butter, melted
Garnish: fresh berries, maple syrup

Sift together flour, baking powder and salt; set aside. With an electric mixer on high speed, beat egg whites until stiff peaks form; set aside. Stir egg yolks, milk and melted butter together and add to flour mixture, stirring just until moistened. Fold in egg whites. Ladle batter by 1/2 cupfuls onto a lightly greased preheated waffle iron; bake according to manufacturer's directions. Garnish as desired.

Sarah Cameron, Maryville, TN

Custardy French Toast

The best French toast you'll ever make! Sit back and enjoy all the compliments.

Serves 6 to 8

6 eggs, beaten
3/4 c. whipping cream
3/4 c. milk
1/4 c. sugar
1/4 t. cinnamon
1 loaf French bread, thickly sliced
2 T. butter, divided
Optional: powdered sugar

In a large shallow bowl, whisk eggs, cream, milk, sugar and cinnamon until well blended. Dip bread slices one at a time into egg mixture, turning to allow both sides to absorb mixture. Melt one tablespoon butter in a cast-iron skillet over medium heat. Cook for about 4 minutes per side, until golden and firm to the touch. Repeat with remaining butter and bread. Dust with powdered sugar, if desired.

Grandma McKindley's Waffles

Barbara Janssen, Park Beach, IL

Light & Fluffy Pancakes

Everyone loves pancakes, but when time is short, pancakes can keep the cook in the kitchen too long! These fluffy pancakes can be made ahead and frozen. They warm up beautifully and everyone is happy!

Makes 6 to 8 servings

1 c. all-purpose flour
2 T. sugar
2 t. baking powder
1/2 t. salt
1 egg, beaten
1 c. milk
2 T. oil

Garnish: fresh raspberries, whipped cream or powdered sugar

Stir together flour, sugar, baking powder and salt. Add egg, milk and oil all at once to flour mixture, stirring until blended but still slightly lumpy. Pour batter onto a hot, lightly greased griddle or heavy skillet, about 1/4 cup each for regular pancakes or one tablespoon for silver dollar pancakes. Cook on both sides until golden, turning when surface is bubbly and edges are slightly dry. Garnish as desired.

★ SIMPLE INGREDIENT SWAP ★ **Did you know you can use mashed bananas for all or part of the liquid in pancake recipes? The end result is extra-moist pancakes loaded with flavor.**

Light & Fluffy Pancakes

Michelle Case, Yardley, PA

Breakfast Berry Parfait

Choose a simple glass dish to present this super-easy breakfast. Or for a fancier look, serve it in parfait glasses or champagne flutes. Choose the flavor of yogurt that your family loves...it all tastes so good!

Makes 3 servings

3/4 c. strawberries, hulled
1/2 c. raspberries
1/4 c. blacberries
1 c. bran & raisin cereal
6-oz. container strawberry yogurt
Garnish: additional fresh berries

Combine berries in a bowl. Top with cereal. Spoon yogurt over berry mixture. Garnish with fresh berries.

Jill Ball, Highland, UT

Apple Pie Oatmeal

This is an easy, healthy and hearty breakfast. Sprinkle a little cinnamon and sugar on top for extra sweetness in the morning.

Makes one serving

1 c. water
6 T. long-cooking oats, uncooked
1 t. brown sugar, packed
2 T. apple, peeled, cored and diced
1/8 t. apple pie spice
Optional: milk

Combine water and oats in a microwave-safe bowl. Cover tightly with plastic wrap, folding back a small edge to allow steam to escape. Microwave on high for 2-1/2 minutes. Stir well. Top with remaining ingredients and milk, if desired.

Breakfast Berry Parfait

Christina Mendoza, Alamogordo, NM

California Omelet

Always a special breakfast, omelets make the quickest and heartiest breakfasts for the entire family...you can personalize each one to include favorite flavors.

Makes 2 servings

1 T. oil
3 to 4 eggs, beaten
1/4 c. milk
salt and pepper to taste
1 avocado, peeled, pitted and sliced
2 green onions, diced
1/2 c. shredded Monterey jack
   cheese

Heat oil in a skillet over medium-low heat. Wisk together eggs, milk, salt and pepper in a bowl; pour into skillet. Cook until eggs are lightly golden on bottom and partially set on top. Sprinkle with remaining ingredients; carefully fold omelet in half so toppings are covered. Reduce heat and cook, uncovered, about 5 to 10 minutes.

★ MAKE IT FOR DINNER ★ Don't just think breakfast...savory dinnertime omelets are delicious and easy. Fill omelets with leftover sautéed vegetables and shredded cheese...scrumptious! Add a basket of multi-grain English muffins and dinner is served.

California Omelet

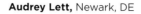

Jennifer Hollingsworth,
Powder Springs, GA

Veggie & Sprouts Bagel

I made this for myself and was amazed at how much I loved it! When my kids saw how much I liked it, they took what I had left and begged me to make more. It's such a fresh-tasting and healthy snack.

Makes one serving

1 mini whole-wheat bagel, halved
   and lightly toasted
1 T. onion & chive flavored cream
   cheese, softened
2 T. alfalfa sprouts
2 slices tomato
2 to 4 cucumber slices
sea salt to taste

Spread each bagel half with cream cheese. Top each half with alfalfa sprouts, one tomato slice and one to 2 cucumber slices. Sprinkle with just a little salt to taste.

Audrey Lett, Newark, DE

Suzanne's Tomato Melt

Start your day with fresh garden flavor...hearty and delicious!

Makes one serving

1/4 c. shredded Cheddar cheese
1 onion bagel or English muffin, split
2 tomato slices
1 T. shredded Parmesan cheese

Sprinkle half the Cheddar cheese over each bagel or English muffin half. Top with a tomato slice. Sprinkle half the Parmesan cheese over each tomato. Broil about 6 inches from heat for 4 to 5 minutes, or until cheese is bubbly.

Veggie & Sprouts Bagel

Beth Kramer, Port Saint Lucie, FL

Flatbread Breakfast Pizza

My teenagers love to whip up these little breakfast pizzas. Sometimes we'll add leftover crispy bacon too...yum!

Makes one serving

1 egg, beaten

1 T. milk

1 brown & serve breakfast sausage link or patty, browned and chopped

6-inch round flatbread

2 T. finely shredded Cheddar cheese

In a greased 2-cup microwave-safe bowl, whisk together egg and milk; stir in sausage. Microwave on high for 30 seconds; use a spoon to push cooked edges toward center. Microwave for 15 to 45 seconds, until egg is almost set. Turn out egg and slice into 4 to 5 pieces; arrange on flatbread. Sprinkle with cheese. Microwave an additional 10 to 15 seconds, until cheese melts.

★ TIME-SAVING SHORTCUT ★ **Out of flatbread? Try this breakfast pizza with pita bread, tortillas or even toast.**

Flatbread Breakfast Pizza

Jo Ann, Gooseberry Patch

Good Morning Blueberry Shake

I enjoy a yummy breakfast shake...
this drink blends up fast and is
so pretty!

Makes 4 servings

2-1/2 c. blueberries
1-1/4 c. apple juice
1 c. frozen vanilla yogurt
1/4 c. milk
3/4 t. cinnamon
Garnish: additional blueberries

Combine all ingredients except
garnish in a blender and process until
smooth. Garnish with additional
blueberries. Serve immediately.

Shirl Parsons, Cape Carteret, NC

Raspberry Cream Smoothies

I have been making these refreshing
smoothies for years. They're a
delicious treat for any time of day!

Makes 8 servings

3 c. frozen raspberries
1 c. banana, cubed and frozen
2 c. orange juice
2 c. frozen vanilla yogurt
2 c. raspberry yogurt
2 t. vanilla extract

In a blender, combine frozen fruit
and remaining ingredients. Process
until smooth; stir, if needed. Pour
into chilled glasses.

★ FREEZE IT ★ **Save bananas**
that are getting too ripe. Peel, cut into
chunks, wrap in plastic wrap and tuck in
the freezer. Later they can be tossed into
smoothies...no thawing needed.

Good Morning Blueberry Shake

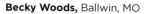

Terri Carr, Lewes, DE

Poached Pesto Eggs

I'm always looking for new ideas for my husband's breakfast. I thought pesto and eggs would be a good combination. He loved it!

Serves one to 2

2 eggs
2 to 3 T. basil pesto sauce
2 slices bread, toasted
2 to 4 slices tomato
Garnish: fresh parsley, chopped

Add 2 inches water to a skillet. Bring to a simmer over high heat. One egg at a time, break eggs into a cup and slide into simmering water. Cook eggs for 3 to 5 minutes, to desired doneness. Spread pesto over toast slices; top with tomato slices. With a slotted spoon, top each slice with an egg. Sprinkle with parsley.

Becky Woods, Ballwin, MO

Smoked Gouda Grits

These smoky and creamy grits are the perfect addition to scrambled eggs and breakfast sausage...yum!

Serves 6 to 8

6 c. chicken broth
2 c. milk
1 t. salt
1/2 t. white pepper
2 c. quick-cooking grits, uncooked
1-2/3 c. shredded smoked Gouda cheese
3 T. butter, softened

Bring broth, milk, salt and pepper to a boil in a large saucepan over medium heat. Gradually whisk in grits. Reduce heat; cover and simmer, stirring occasionally, about 5 minutes or until thickened. Add cheese and butter; stir until melted.

Poached Pesto Eggs

Chicken Taco Salad, Page 108

CHAPTER THREE

Time For a Quick Lunch

Tomato Sandwiches, Page 120

Broccoli-Garlic Lemon Soup, Page 94

Carly St. Clair, Lynnwood, WA

American-Style Pho

On a cold day, I made this soup for my son and myself. We loved it so much we just had to share it!

Makes 6 servings

3 3-oz. pkgs. chicken-flavored ramen
noodles, uncooked
6 c. water
12-oz. can chicken
6 green onions, diced
1/3 head cabbage, sliced into long
thin strips, or 2 to 3 c. shredded
coleslaw mix

In a large saucepan, cook ramen noodles in water according to package instructions. Stir in seasoning packets; do not drain. Add chicken with juices; heat through. To serve, divide onions and cabbage among 6 soup bowls; reserve some of each for garnish. Ladle soup into bowls. Garnish with reserved onions and cabbage.

Angie Womack, Cave City, AR

Mom's Beef Vegetable Soup

After my oldest son got married, he would call and ask me how to make different dishes. When I gave him this recipe, he said, "Mom, this is easy...I always thought you were really working hard when you made this soup!" No more shortcuts for him!

Makes 8 servings

1-1/2 lbs. ground beef
1/2 c. onion, diced
1 clove garlic, minced
2 8-oz. cans tomato sauce
14-1/2 oz. can Italian-style diced
tomatoes
29-oz. can mixed stew vegetables
2 c. water
salt and pepper to taste
Garnish: shredded Cheddar cheese

Brown beef in a soup pot over medium heat; drain. Add onion and garlic; cook until tender. Add tomato sauce, undrained tomatoes and mixed vegetables, water and seasonings. Bring to a boil; lower heat and simmer for 30 minutes. More water may be added for a thinner soup. Serve topped with cheese.

American-Style Pho

Barbara Cooper, Orion, IL

Pulled Chicken & Slaw Sandwiches

These sandwiches are super easy because you start with a roasted chicken from the deli. The creamy slaw adds a nice crunch...yum!

Makes 6 sandwiches

1 c. favorite barbecue sauce
1 c. catsup
1/2 c. water
1 t. lemon juice
2/3 c. brown sugar, packed
1 deli roast chicken, boned and
   shredded
6 buns, split
Garnish: deli coleslaw

In a large saucepan, combine barbecue sauce, catsup, water, lemon juice and brown sugar. Stir well; add chicken. Cook over medium heat until mixture is heated through. Serve on buns; spoon slaw over chicken.

Donna Jackson, Brandon, MS

Oh-So-Easy Chili

Standard football viewing fare at our house in the fall. Add some buttered cornbread and you've got a fantastic meal! The ingredients can also be put in a slow cooker to simmer all day on low.

Makes 4 servings

1 lb. ground beef
1/2 c. onion, chopped
16-oz. can kidney beans
16-oz. can diced tomatoes
8-oz. can tomato sauce
1 T. chili powder
1 t. salt
Optional: shredded Cheddar cheese,
   sour cream

In a large skillet over medium heat, brown beef and onion; drain. Stir in undrained beans and tomatoes, tomato sauce and seasonings. Cover and simmer for 30 minutes, stirring occasionally. Top individual servings with cheese or sour cream, if desired.

Pulled Chicken & Slaw Sandwiches

Lucy Straw, Nottingham, UK

Broccoli-Garlic Lemon Soup

This recipe is based on a soup served at an inn where Prince William enjoyed the cuisine. This soup is best made with all fresh ingredients, but if you cannot get them, make it anyway!

Makes 4 servings

1 T. butter
2 to 3 cloves garlic, minced
1 lb. broccoli, cut into flowerets
zest of 1 lemon
juice of 1/2 lemon
salt to taste
3 c. boiling water
pepper to taste
Garnish: plain yogurt

In a large saucepan over medium heat, melt butter. Add garlic; sauté lightly. Add broccoli, lemon zest, lemon juice and salt. Stir in boiling water. Simmer gently until broccoli is tender but still bright green. Purée mixture in a food processor or blender; pour into warmed bowls. Add pepper; garnish with swirls of yogurt. Serve at once.

★ FREEZE IT ★ Freeze summer vegetables to enjoy year 'round. Create a "stew bag" by combining corn, carrots, celery, onion, broccoli, tomatoes and potatoes for hearty stews and soups.

Broccoli-Garlic Lemon Soup

Kisha Landeros, Pacific, MO

Hoagie Hamburger Boats

This is a dish my brother and I would always request! My mom made these sandwiches for us for busy afternoons and school nights. Simple to make, very filling and easy clean-up.

Makes 6 servings

6 hoagie rolls
1 to 1-1/2 lbs. ground beef
10-3/4 oz. can cream of
   mushroom soup
salt and pepper to taste
6 slices American cheese

Slice off the tops of hoagie rolls. Pull out the centers of rolls to create "boats." Set aside tops and bread pieces. In a skillet over medium heat, brown beef; drain. Stir in soup and bread pieces; season with salt and pepper. Simmer for a few minutes, until heated through. Place rolls on a baking sheet; spoon beef mixture into rolls. Add cheese slices; replace tops onto rolls. Bake at 400 degrees for 10 to 15 minutes, until cheese is melted.

★ FOOD FLEX ★ It pays to have flexible dinner plans. If you were going to use ground beef in a sandwich or casserole recipe for dinner but ground turkey is on sale today, why not use that instead?

Hoagie Hamburger Boats

Amy Thomason-Hunt, Traphill, NC

Sandwich on a Stick

Here's a simple snack to make for a picnic or party. Adjust the ingredients and quantity to suit your family's tastes.

Makes 8 servings

1/2 lb. deli roast chicken, cubed
1/2 lb. deli roast turkey, cubed
1/2 lb. deli baked ham, cubed
1/2 lb. Cheddar cheese, cut into cubes
4 c. bread, cut into cubes
1 pt. cherry tomatoes
4 dill pickles, cut into chunks
8 wooden skewers
Garnish: mustard, spicy brown
    mustard, mayonnaise

Alternate all ingredients except condiments onto skewers. Garnish as desired.

Arleela Connor, Leopold, IN

Toasted Ham & Cheese

Serve these buttery sandwiches with a side of potato chips and a crisp dill pickle, or a cup of tomato bisque... pure comfort!

Makes 4 servings

2-1/2 T. butter, softened
8 slices sourdough bread
4 slices Colby cheese
1/2 lb. shaved deli ham
4 slices Swiss cheese

Spread butter on one side of each slice of bread. Arrange 4 bread slices, buttered-side down, in a cast-iron skillet over medium-high heat. Top with one slice Colby cheese, desired amount of ham and one slice Swiss cheese. Add remaining bread slices, buttered-side up. Grill sandwiches on both sides until golden and cheese melts.

★ FINGER FOOD ★ Sandwich sushi is sure to be a hit for picnics, after-school snacking, or in lunchboxes. Spread tortillas with cream cheese and layer on sliced deli meat and spinach leaves, or other favorite foods...there are lots of possibilities. Roll up tightly and slice into easy-to-handle pieces.

Sandwich on a Stick

Alice Hardin, Antioch, CA

Yummy Chicken-Leek Soup

Savory and packed with veggies... great for chilly days!

Makes 4 servings

2 t. olive oil
2 leeks, white and light green
   parts thinly sliced
1 onion, chopped
1 carrot, peeled and thinly sliced
2 skinless chicken thighs
3 c. reduced-sodium chicken
   broth
1 T. fresh parsley, chopped
1/2 t. salt
1/4 t. pepper

Heat oil in a large non-stick saucepan over medium heat. Cook leeks, onion and carrot until softened, stirring occasionally, about 10 minutes. Add chicken and broth; bring to a boil. Reduce heat and simmer, covered, until chicken is cooked through, about 20 minutes. Transfer chicken to a cutting board; cool slightly. Discard bones; dice chicken and return to soup. Stir in seasonings. Heat through, 2 to 3 minutes.

Lisa McClelland, Columbus, OH

Tangy Salmon Cream Soup

I created this recipe for a meal that's quick, yet fancy enough to set before company when unexpected guests come for the evening.

Makes 4 servings

8-oz. pkg. cream cheese, cubed and
   softened
1 c. milk
14-oz. can chicken broth
2-1/2 t. Dijon mustard
1-1/2 t. fresh dill, chopped
1 c. frozen peas
2 green onions, sliced
12-oz. pkg. smoked salmon, flaked
Optional: chopped fresh chives

In a saucepan over medium-low heat, combine all ingredients except salmon and chives. Cook, stirring often, until cheese is melted and soup is smooth. Stir in salmon; heat through. Sprinkle with chives, if desired.

Yummy Chicken-Leek Soup

Carol Hickman, Kingsport, TN

Island Chicken Salad

Pile this delicious chicken salad high on a lettuce leaf or serve on fresh croissants for a quick sandwich.

Makes 4 servings

10-oz. can chunk white chicken, drained
8-oz. can crushed pineapple, drained
2 stalks celery, diced
1/2 c. cream cheese, softened
2 T. mayonnaise
Garnish: sliced almonds

In a large bowl, combine all ingredients except almonds. Mix together until well blended. Cover and chill; serve topped with almonds. Makes 4 servings.

Kathy Milliga, Mira, Loma, CA

Sesame-Asparagus Salad

Our family loves this salad in springtime when asparagus is fresh... it tastes terrific and is easy to prepare.

Serves 4 to 6

1-1/2 lbs. asparagus, cut diagonally into 2-inch pieces
3 T. toasted sesame oil
1 t. white wine vinegar
4 t. soy sauce
2-1/2 T. sugar or honey
4 t. toasted sesame seed

Bring a large saucepan of water to a boil over high heat. Add asparagus; cook for 2 to 3 minutes, just until crisp-tender. Immediately drain asparagus; rinse with cold water until asparagus is completely cooled. Drain again; pat dry. Cover and refrigerate until chilled, about one hour. In a small bowl, whisk together remaining ingredients; cover and refrigerate. At serving time, drizzle asparagus with dressing; toss to coat.

Island Chicken Salad

Jill Ross, Pickerington, OH

BBQ Chicken Calzones

With a recipe this easy, it's a pleasure to have my children lend a hand in the kitchen!

Makes 4 servings

12-oz. tube refrigerated pizza dough
3 c. cooked chicken, diced
1 c. barbecue sauce
1 c. shredded mozzarella cheese
1 egg, beaten
1 t. water

On a floured surface, roll dough to 1/2-inch thickness; cut into 2 rectangles and place on ungreased baking sheets. In a bowl, combine chicken and barbecue sauce. For each calzone, spoon half the chicken mixture onto one half of the dough. Top with half the cheese. Fold over dough and seal the edges. Mix together egg and water. Use a pastry brush to brush egg mixture over each calzone; use a knife to cut 3 slits in the tops. Bake at 400 degrees for 25 minutes, or until golden.

★ HANDY TIP ★ You may be able to purchase fresh, unbaked pizza dough from your favorite local pizza shop. It's also often found in the refrigerator case at the supermarket.

BBQ Chicken Calzones

Wendy Perry, Lorton, VA

Buffalo Chicken Salad Sliders

These quick-to-make sandwiches are perfect when you have a big, hungry crowd!

Makes 8 sandwiches

3/4 c. mayonnaise
1/4 c. sour cream
2 T. hot pepper sauce
1 t. garlic powder
1/2 t. salt
3 c. cooked chicken, diced
3/4 c. celery, diced
1/2 c. sweet onion, diced
8 potato dinner rolls, split
Optional: lettuce leaves, sliced
    tomato and cucumber

In a bowl, combine mayonnaise, sour cream, hot sauce and seasonings until well mixed. Stir in chicken, celery and onion. Fill sliced rolls with chicken mixture; garnish, if desired.

Andrew Neymeyer, Des Moines, IA

Pepperoni Pizza Sandwiches

This recipe could not be any easier, or more delicious!

Makes 6 servings

3 bagels, halved
1 c. pizza sauce
8-oz. pkg. shredded Italian-style
    shredded cheese
5-oz. pkg. mini pepperoni slices

Lay bagel halves cut-side up on a baking sheet. Spread a thin layer of pizza sauce on each bagel. Sprinkle a layer of cheese on the sauce. Top with slices of pepperoni. Top with more cheese, if desired. Bake at 375 degrees for about 10 minutes, until cheese is melted. Serve immediately.

★ SAVVY SWAP ★ Why not try Pepperoni Pizza Sandwiches with a different Italian deli meat? There's plenty to choose from...salami, soppresatta, prosciutto, capicola, mortadella... and all of them are so tasty!

Buffalo Chicken Salad Sliders

Abby Snay, San Francisco, CA

Chicken Taco Salad

Such a colorful and tasty taco lunch!

Makes 8 servings

8 6-inch flour tortillas
2 c. cooked chicken breast, shredded
2 t. taco seasoning mix
1/2 c. water
2 c. lettuce, shredded
1/2 c. black beans, drained
**   and rinsed**
1 c. shredded Cheddar cheese
1/2 c. green onion, sliced
1/2 c. canned corn, drained
2-1/4 oz. can sliced black olives,
**   drained**
1/2 avocado, pitted, peeled and cubed
Garnish: fresh salsa

Microwave tortillas on high setting for one minute, or until softened. Press each tortilla into an ungreased jumbo muffin cup to form a bowl shape. Bake at 350 degrees for 10 minutes; cool. Combine chicken, taco seasoning and water in a skillet over medium heat. Cook, stirring frequently, until blended, about 5 minutes. Divide lettuce among tortilla bowls. Top with chicken and other ingredients, garnishing with salsa.

★ DOUBLE BATCH ★ Cook once, eat twice! Make a double batch of baked chicken, meatloaf, meatballs or taco beef, then freeze half. On a busy night, how wonderful to simply pull dinner from the freezer, reheat and serve.

Chicken Taco Salad

Lois Carswell, Kennesaw, GA

Confetti Corn & Rice Salad

This colorful salad is a favorite at our family gatherings and barbecues, especially during the summer when we can use fresh-picked sweet corn...yum!

Makes 8 servings

4 ears corn, husked
1-1/2 c. cooked rice
1 red onion, thinly sliced
1 green pepper, halved and thinly
  sliced
1 pt. cherry tomatoes, halved
Optional: 1 jalapeño pepper, thinly
  sliced

Boil or grill ears of corn until tender; let cool. With a sharp knife, cut corn from cob in "planks." In a serving bowl, combine rice, red onion, green pepper, tomatoes and jalapeño pepper, if using. Mix in corn, keeping some corn planks for top. Drizzle with Simple Dressing. Serve at room temperature or refrigerate overnight before serving. Add reserved corn on top.

Simple Dressing:

2 T. red wine vinegar
2 T. olive oil
salt and pepper to taste

Whisk all ingredients together.

Claudia Olsen, Chester, NJ

Penne & Goat Cheese Salad

One of my husband's favorite pasta dishes...it's just a little different from most. Try arugula for a slightly spicy taste or feta cheese if you prefer it to goat cheese. This makes a great main dish for a light dinner.

Makes 8 servings

12-oz. pkg. penne pasta, uncooked
1 T. garlic, minced
1/4 c. mayonnaise
4-oz. pkg. goat cheese, diced
1/2 c. sun-dried tomatoes packed in
  oil, drained and oil reserved
2 c. baby spinach, coarsely chopped

Cook pasta according to package directions; drain and rinse with cold water. In a large bowl, combine pasta with garlic, mayonnaise and goat cheese. Finely chop tomatoes and add along with spinach; mix gently. Stir in reserved oil from tomatoes, one tablespoon at a time, until ingredients are nicely coated. Serve at room temperature, or cover and chill.

Confetti Corn & Rice Salad

Gretchen Ham, Pine City, NY

Quick & Easy Tomato Soup

Fresh basil really makes this soup special. The flavors get even better when it is warmed up the next day!

Makes 10 servings

1/2 c. butter, sliced
1 c. fresh basil, chopped
2 28-oz. cans crushed tomatoes
2 cloves garlic, minced
1 qt. half-and-half
salt and pepper to taste
Garnish: fresh parsley, sliced cherry
    tomatoes, croutons

In a large saucepan, melt butter over medium heat. Add basil; sauté for 2 minutes. Add tomatoes with juice and garlic; reduce heat and simmer for 20 minutes. Remove from heat; let cool slightly. Working in batches, transfer tomato mixture to a blender and purée. Strain into a separate saucepan and add half-and-half, mixing very well. Reheat soup over medium-low heat; add salt and pepper to taste. Garnish as desired.

★ FRESH HERBS ★ Create an Italian herb garden right outside the kitchen door! Plant basil, oregano, parsley and any other herbs you like. In no time at all you'll have fresh herbs available for every dish!

Quick & Easy Tomato Soup

Vickie, Gooseberry Patch

Pepper Steak Sammie

Everyone loves a steak sandwich and this one won't disappoint...enjoy!

Makes 4 sandwiches

1 to 1-1/4 lbs. beef sirloin or ribeye
  steak
2 green peppers, thinly sliced
1 onion, sliced
1 T. oil
salt and pepper to taste
1/4 c. garlic butter, softened
4 French rolls, split and toasted

Grill or broil steak to desired doneness; set aside. Sauté green peppers and onion in hot oil in a skillet over medium heat until crisp-tender; drain. Slice steak thinly; add to skillet and heat through. Sprinkle with salt and pepper. Spread butter over cut sides of rolls. Spoon steak mixture onto bottom halves of rolls; cover with tops.

Barb Bargdill, Gooseberry Patch

Cheesy Tuna Melts

It's the sweet raisin bread and chopped apple that make these sandwiches stand out from all the rest.

Makes 12 servings

1 T. oil
1 c. apple, cored and chopped
3 T. onion, chopped
7-oz. can albacore tuna, drained
1/4 c. chopped walnuts
1/4 c. light mayonnaise
2 t. lemon juice
1/8 t. salt
1/8 t. pepper
6 slices raisin bread, toasted and
  halved diagonally
6 slices sharp Cheddar cheese,
  halved diagonally

Heat oil in a skillet over medium heat; add apple and onion. Cook, stirring occasionally, about 5 minutes, until tender. Remove from heat; transfer to a bowl. Stir in tuna, walnuts, mayonnaise, lemon juice, salt and pepper. Place toast slices on an ungreased baking sheet. Top with tuna mixture and a slice of cheese. Broil 4 to 5 inches from heat for 3 to 4 minutes, or until cheese begins to melt.

Pepper Steak Sammie

Julie Ann Perkins, Anderson, IN

Green Goddess Bacon Salad

This salad is perfect for a main-dish salad because it has great protein in it. Green Goddess salad dressing was so popular mid-century and now it is so popular again. We never stopped serving or loving it!

Makes 6 servings

7 eggs, hard-boiled, peeled and sliced
7 to 12 slices bacon, chopped and
  crisply cooked
3 c. deli roast chicken, shredded
6 to 8 c. baby spinach
1 red pepper, chopped
Optional: 1 bunch green onions,
  sliced
Green Goddess salad dressing to taste

In a large salad bowl, combine eggs, bacon, chicken and vegetables; mix well. Pass salad dressing at the table so guests may add it to taste.

Brenda Huey, Geneva, IN

Log Cabin Salad

My mom, Iris, lives in a little log cabin by a lake. I named this salad recipe for her. We love the rice, fruit and greens combination.

Makes 15 servings

2 lbs. salad greens
1/4 lb. bacon, crisply cooked and
  crumbled
1 c. chopped pecans
6-oz. pkg. long-grain and wild rice,
  cooked
1 c. crumbled blue cheese
2-1/2 c. blueberries, divided
1 c. favorite poppy seed salad dressing

Arrange greens in a large serving bowl. Toss with bacon, pecans, rice, cheese and 1/2 cup blueberries. Mash remaining blueberries and whisk with salad dressing. Drizzle over individual servings.

★ DO IT YOURSELF ★ To make your own Green Goddess dressing, simply combine 2 cups mayonnaise, one tablespoon tarragon vinegar, 2 teaspoons diced fresh parsley, 2 teaspoons diced fresh chives, one teaspoon diced fresh tarragon, and one diced green onion. Combine all ingredients in a blender or food processor and process until smooth. Thin to desired consistency with a little bit of milk, if needed. Keep refrigerated. Makes about 2 cups.

Green Goddess Bacon Salad

Irene Whatling, West Des Moines, IA

Peanut Butter Apple-Bacon Sandwich

My family loves this grilled sandwich. I make it for lunch once a week! Sometimes I add some mild Cheddar cheese instead of the peanut butter.

Makes 4 sandwiches

8 slices applewood smoked bacon
8 slices whole-grain bread
1/4 c. peach preserves
1 to 2 apples, cored and thinly sliced
1/4 c. creamy peanut butter
2 to 3 T. butter, softened and divided

In a skillet over medium heat, cook bacon until crisp; drain bacon on paper towels. Spread 4 slices of bread with preserves; layer apple and bacon slices over preserves. Spread remaining bread slices with peanut butter; close sandwiches. Spread tops of sandwiches with half of butter. Place sandwiches butter-side down on a griddle over medium heat. Spread remaining butter on unbuttered side of sandwiches. Cook 2 to 3 minutes per side, until bread is toasted and sandwiches are heated through. Serve warm.

★ BETTER BACON ★ Crispy bacon makes any sandwich a winner! Lay slices on a jelly-roll pan and bake at 350 degrees for 15 to 20 minutes, until they're as crisp as you like. Drain well on paper towels.

Peanut Butter Apple-Bacon Sandwich

Diane Long, Delaware, OH

Tomato Sandwiches

Use garden tomatoes warm from the summer sun to make these sandwiches extra special.

Makes 5 servings

10 slices pumpernickel bread
3 tomatoes, thickly sliced
10 sprigs fresh watercress
1 red onion, sliced
1 green pepper, sliced
1/4 t. pepper
1 T. mayonnaise

Top each of 5 bread slices with tomato slices, 2 sprigs of watercress, a slice of onion and 2 slices of green pepper. Sprinkle with salt and pepper. Spread mayonnaise over remaining bread slices and top sandwiches.

Kathy Majeske, Denver, PA

Brown Sugar Barbecue Sandwiches

Need a meal for the whole soccer team? This recipe is just the thing! It's quick because there's no need to brown the beef first.

Makes 12 servings

1 c. water
3/4 c. catsup
2 T. brown sugar, packed
1 onion, chopped
2 T. mustard
1 T. chili powder
2 t. salt
1 t. pepper
2 lbs. lean ground beef
12 sandwich buns, split

In a large cast-iron skillet, mix all ingredients except beef and buns. Bring to a boil over medium heat. Add uncooked beef, breaking up with a spatula; simmer for 30 minutes. Spoon onto buns.

Tomato Sandwiches

Cheri Maxwell, Gulf Breeze, FL

Caribbean Chicken Salad

Try grilling the chicken on a countertop grill for a different flavor.

Makes 4 servings

1/2 c. honey-mustard salad dressing
1 t. lime zest
4 boneless, skinless chicken breasts
1 T. Jamaican jerk seasoning
1 T. oil
2 10-oz. pkgs. mixed salad greens
2 mangoes, peeled, pitted and diced

Stir together salad dressing and lime zest; cover and chill. Sprinkle chicken with seasoning. Heat oil over medium heat in a large skillet. Add chicken; cook 6 minutes per side until golden and no longer pink. Slice chicken thinly. Arrange salad greens on 4 plates; top with chicken and mangoes. Drizzle with dressing.

Tori Willis, Champaign, IL

Yiayia's Chicken Pitas

Though not exactly like my grandma's famous Greek sandwiches, they're pretty darn close!

Makes 4 servings

1/2 c. plain yogurt
1/4 c. cucumber, finely chopped
1/2 t. dill weed
1/4 t. dried mint, crushed
4 pita bread rounds
4 lettuce leaves
2 c. cooked chicken, cubed
1 tomato, thinly sliced
1/3 c. crumbled feta cheese

In a small bowl, stir together yogurt, cucumber, dill weed and mint; set aside. For each sandwich, layer a pita with lettuce, chicken, tomato and cheese. Spoon yogurt mixture on top. Roll up pita and secure with a wooden toothpick. Serve immediately.

Caribbean Chicken Salad

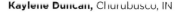

Darbara Durke, Gulfport, MS

Lemon-Herb Chicken Salad

The lemon-herb dressing makes this chicken salad just a little different. It is really very filling and I like to make it pretty by serving it on sliced tomatoes. It's especially good with a rustic brown bread.

Serves 4 to 6

2 boneless, skinless chicken breasts, cooked and diced
1/4 c. mayonnaise
1/4 c. plain yogurt
1 T. fresh dill, chopped
2 t. lemon juice
1/2 t. lemon zest
1/4 t. salt

Place chicken in a serving bowl; set aside. Combine remaining ingredients; mix well and toss with chicken. Chill before serving.

Kaylene Duncan, Churubusco, IN

Aloha Sandwiches

This sandwich couldn't be any easier to prepare...just toss together all the ingredients and serve!

Makes 4 to 8 servings

3 10-oz. cans chicken, drained
1 c. celery, chopped
1 c. seedless grapes, halved
1 c. mayonnaise-type salad dressing
1/2 c. chopped pecans
1/4 c. whipping cream
1 t. salt
12-oz. pkg. Hawaiian rolls, split

Combine all ingredients except salt and rolls; toss to mix well. Sprinkle with salt; blend well and spoon over rolls.

Lemon-Herb Chicken Salad

Judy Bailey, Des Moines, IA

Smokin' Hot Grilled-Cheese Sandwiches

We love grilled cheese, but I like to give my family healthy choices. This is a great combination of flavors and a little more healthy than the usual grilled cheese.

Makes 4 sandwiches

8 slices whole-grain rye bread
3 t. butter, softened and divided
2 tomatoes, sliced
1/4 lb. Pepper Jack cheese, sliced
1 green pepper, sliced

Spread 4 slices bread on one side with half the butter. Top with tomato, cheese, green pepper and another slice of bread; spread remaining butter on outside of sandwiches. Heat a large skillet over medium heat. Cook sandwiches for 2 to 3 minutes, until bread is golden and cheese begins to melt. Turn over; press down slightly with a spatula. Cook until golden.

Jennifer Catterino, Pasadena, MD

Simple Sloppy Joes

These sandwiches will be a winner with the family for their flavor and with Mom for their ease!

Serves 6 to 8

1 lb. ground beef
1 onion, chopped
1 c. catsup
1/4 c. water
2 T. Worcestershire sauce
1/4 t. salt
1/4 t. pepper
6 to 8 sandwich buns, split
Garnish: dill pickle slices

Cook ground beef and onion in a large skillet over medium-high heat, stirring until beef crumbles and is no longer pink; drain. Stir in catsup, water, Worcestershire sauce, salt and pepper; simmer 20 minutes, stirring frequently. Spoon onto buns; top with dill pickle slices.

Smokin' Hot Grilled-Cheese Sandwiches

Tammy Rowe, Bellevue, OH

Asian Chicken Salad

For some variety, make lettuce wraps using these same ingredients. Separate the lettuce into large leaves, layer with toppings and drizzle with dressing...wrap and eat!

Makes 4 servings

1 head lettuce, shredded
2 to 3 boneless, skinless chicken
  breasts, cooked and shredded
1/2 c. snow peas
1 bunch green onions, chopped
2 T. slivered almonds
5-oz. can chow mein noodles
2 T. poppy seed

Combine all ingredients in a large salad bowl. Pour dressing over top and toss well. Serve immediately.

Dressing:
1/4 c. vinegar
2 T. sugar
1/2 t. salt
1/2 t. pepper

Whisk ingredients together until well combined.

★ ASIAN ZING ★ For a little extra zing, drizzle this dressing on your Asian Chicken Salad. In a small bowl, combine 3 tablespoons lemon juice, 2 tablespoons tahini, 1 tablespoon sugar, 2 teaspoons soy sauce, 1 teaspoon peeled minced ginger, 1/2 teaspoon minced garlic, and 1/8 teaspoon pepper. Whisk until well blended.

Asian Chicken Salad

Brown Butter Gnocchi & Spinach, Page 140

CHAPTER FOUR

Simple Suppers & Sides

Deep-Dish Skillet Pizza, Page 154

Marty's Special Burgers, Page 162

Cathy Hillier, Salt Lake City, UT

Mini Turkey Pot Pies

My kids love to help me make these little pot pies over Thanksgiving weekend with leftovers from the big Turkey Day meal.

Serves 4 to 6, one to 2 mini pot pies each

1-1/2 c. cooked turkey, cubed
10-3/4 oz. can cream of chicken soup
1-1/2 c. frozen mixed vegetables, thawed
1/2 c. cooked potato, diced
12-oz. tube refrigerated biscuits
1/2 c. shredded Cheddar cheese

Combine turkey, soup, vegetables and potatoes in a saucepan. Simmer over medium-low heat for 5 minutes. Meanwhile, spray 10 muffin cups with non-stick vegetable spray. Flatten biscuits slightly; press into the bottoms and up the sides of muffin cups. Divide turkey mixture among cups; gently press down. Top with cheese. Bake at 350 degrees for 15 minutes, or until golden and cheese is melted. Cool in muffin tin on a wire rack for 5 minutes before removing.

★ EXTRA FLAVOR ★ Fresh, green herbs like basil, dill and sage can be chopped and pressed right into biscuit dough for a pot pie. Lay herbs on the dough and gently press in with your fingers or a rolling pin for extra flavor.

Mini Turkey Pot Pies

Cynthia Varennes, Ontario, Canada

Mom's Meat Rice

My mom used to make this easy recipe often. The whole family loved it and and she knew there would never be any leftovers. I finally got her recipe and now my little family is enjoying it too!

Serves 4 to 6

1 lb. ground beef
3 green, red and/or yellow peppers, chopped
1 sweet onion, chopped
1 T. canola oil
3 c. cooked rice
salt and pepper to taste

Brown beef in a skillet over medium heat; drain and remove to a bowl. In the same skillet, cook peppers and onion in oil; drain. Add beef and cooked rice to vegetables; season with salt and pepper. Warm together over low heat until hot and bubbly.

Alma Meyers, Guernsey, WY

Quick Salisbury Steak

Add a side of mashed potatoes for a hearty, filling dinner!

Makes 4 servings

1 lb. ground beef
1-1/2 oz. pkg. onion soup mix
2 eggs, beaten
2 10-3/4 oz. cans golden mushroom soup

In a large bowl, combine beef, soup mix and eggs; mix well and form into 4 patties. Place patties in an ungreased 13"x9" baking pan; cover with soup. Bake at 350 degrees for 35 minutes, or until patties are no longer pink in the center.

Mom's Meat Rice

Cecilia Ollivares, Santa Paula, CA

Curried Chicken with Mango

I love dishes like this one that don't take too long to make and have a unique flavor. This recipe is delicious and speedy...perfect served with a side of naan flatbread.

Serves 4 to 6

2 T. oil
4 boneless, skinless chicken breasts, cooked and sliced
13.6-oz. can coconut milk
1 c. mango, peeled, pitted and cubed
2 to 3 T. curry powder
cooked jasmine rice

Heat oil in a large skillet over medium heat. Cook chicken in oil until golden and warmed through. Stir in milk, mango and curry powder. Simmer for 10 minutes, stirring occasionally, or until slightly thickened. Serve over cooked rice.

Michelle Waddington, New Bedford, MA

Baked Crumbed Haddock

Delicious! Serve with mac & cheese and steamed broccoli for a down-home dinner.

Makes 8 servings

2 5-1/2 oz. pkgs. onion & garlic croutons
1/4 c. butter, melted
3 lbs. haddock fillets
Optional: lemon slices

Finely grind croutons in a food processor. Toss together croutons and butter. Place fish in a lightly greased 13"x9" baking pan. Sprinkle crouton mixture over fish. Bake, uncovered, at 350 degrees for 20 to 25 minutes, until fish flakes easily with a fork. Top fish with lemon slices, if desired.

Curried Chicken with Mango

Diane Cohen, Breinigsville, PA

Italian Sausage & Potato Roast

So easy...everything is baked on a sheet pan!

Makes 4 servings

3/4 lb. redskin potatoes, cut into
  quarters
1 yellow pepper, sliced into strips
1 green pepper, sliced into strips
1/2 sweet onion, sliced
1 T. olive oil
1 t. garlic salt or garlic powder
1/4 t. dried oregano
pepper to taste
1 lb. Italian pork sausage, cut into
  chunks

In a large bowl, toss vegetables with olive oil and seasonings. Line a large rimmed baking sheet with aluminum foil; lightly mist with non-stick vegetable spray. Spread vegetables on baking sheet. Place sausage chunks among vegetables. Bake, uncovered, at 450 degrees until sausage is cooked through and vegetables are tender, about 30 minutes, stirring twice during baking.

★ SAVVY SWAP ★ No Italian pork sausage on hand? Chop up some thick slices of cooked deli ham to use instead. Deli turkey, chicken and even roast beef can be used in place of cooked meats in recipes...what a timesaver!

Italian Sausage & Potato Roast

Chad Rutan, Columbus, OH

Brown Butter Gnocchi & Spinach

A super-simple dish to toss together on a weeknight. Take a few basic ingredients plus just a little time and you've got yourself a great-tasting dish!

Makes 4 servings

16-oz. pkg. refrigerated gnocchi
    pasta, uncooked
2 T. butter
2 T. pine nuts
2 cloves garlic, minced
1/2 lb. fresh spinach, torn
1/4 t. salt
1/4 t. pepper
1/4 c. grated Parmesan cheese

Cook pasta according to package directions; drain. Meanwhile, melt butter in a large skillet over medium heat. Add pine nuts to skillet. Cook, stirring constantly, for 3 minutes, or until butter and nuts are golden. Add garlic to skillet; cook for one minute. Add pasta and spinach. Cook, stirring constantly, for one minute, or until spinach wilts. Sprinkle with salt and pepper; stir in cheese.

Irene Robinson, Cincinnati, OH

Lemony Broccoli

A tang of lemon with fresh broccoli... a winning combination.

Makes 6 servings

1-1/2 lbs. broccoli, cut into spears
1/2 clove garlic, minced
2 T. olive oil
2 T. lemon juice

Add broccoli to a saucepan with a small amount of water. Over medium-high heat, cook broccoli 6 to 8 minutes, until crisp-tender. Drain; place broccoli in a bowl and set aside. In the same pan, sauté garlic in oil over medium heat, until tender. Add lemon juice; mix well. Pour over broccoli, tossing gently to blend.

★ HOT TIP ★ Super-special bread to go with this Brown Butter Gnocchi & Spinach! Cut a loaf of French bread into slices, stopping just short of the bottom crust. Combine 3/4 cup shredded Cheddar cheese, 1/2 cup butter, 1/4 cup chopped fresh parsley, one teaspoon paprika and 3 to 4 cloves minced garlic and then spread mixture between slices. Wrap up in aluminum foil and heat in a 350-degree oven for about 15 minutes. Tasty!

Brown Butter Gnocchi & Spinach

J.J. Presley, Portland, TX

Cheesy Sausage-Potato Casserole

Add some fresh green beans too, if you like.

Serves 6 to 8

3 to 4 potatoes, peeled and sliced
2 8-oz. links pork sausage, sliced into 2-inch lengths
1 onion, chopped
1/2 c. butter, sliced
1 c. shredded Cheddar cheese

Layer potatoes, sausage and onion in a 13"x9" baking pan sprayed with non-stick vegetable spray. Dot with butter; sprinkle with cheese. Bake at 350 degrees for 1-1/2 hours.

Jessica Wantland, Napoleon, OH

Chicken Parmesan

Just six ingredients, but so yummy! Jazz it up with your favorite flavor of pasta sauce...there are lots to choose from.

Makes 4 servings

1 egg, beaten
3/4 c. Italian-seasoned dry bread crumbs
4 boneless, skinless chicken breasts
26-oz. jar pasta sauce
1 c. shredded mozzarella cheese
cooked spaghetti

Place egg and bread crumbs in separate shallow dishes. Dip chicken into egg, then into bread crumbs. Arrange chicken in a greased 13"x9" baking pan. Bake, uncovered, at 400 degrees for 30 minutes. Spoon pasta sauce over chicken and top with cheese. Bake another 15 minutes, or until chicken juices run clear. Serve chicken and sauce over spaghetti.

Cheesy Sausage-Potato Casserole

Tara Horton, Delaware, OH

Chicken Pesto Primo

One summer I grew basil in my garden and froze batches of homemade pesto in ice cube trays. I made up this recipe to use that yummy pesto. When asparagus isn't in season, I'll toss in some broccoli flowerets...it's just as tasty!

Makes 4 servings

8-oz. pkg. rotini pasta, uncooked
2 c. cooked chicken, cubed
1 c. asparagus, steamed and cut into
   1-inch pieces
2 T. basil pesto sauce
1/4 to 1/2 c. chicken broth

Cook pasta according to package directions; drain. In a skillet over medium heat, combine chicken, asparagus, pesto, cooked pasta and 1/4 cup chicken broth. Cook and stir until heated through, adding more broth as needed.

Barbara Bower, Orville, OH

Easy-As-1-2-3 Chicken Bake

Serve with steamed broccoli or asparagus.

Makes 8 servings

3/4 c. corn flake cereal, crushed
3/4 c. grated Parmesan cheese
1-oz. pkg. Italian salad dressing mix
8 boneless, skinless chicken breasts
1/3 c. butter, melted

Mix cereal, Parmesan cheese and salad dressing mix together; coat chicken with mixture. Place in a single layer in a greased 13"x9" baking pan. Sprinkle remaining crumbs on top; drizzle with butter. Bake at 350 degrees for 45 minutes or until juices run clear when chicken is pierced with a fork.

★ MIX IT UP ★ Mix up a Chicken Pesto Primo by substituting different types of pasta. Check out the pasta aisle for bowties, penne, wagon wheels or shells.

Chicken Pesto Primo

Regina Wickline, Pebble Beach, CA

Tortellini with Artichokes & Roasted Peppers

We love this fresh-tasting dish that can be made year 'round from pantry items.

Makes 4 servings

8-oz. pkg. cheese tortellini, uncooked
2 T. butter
2 T. olive oil
2 6-oz. jars marinated artichoke hearts, drained
12-oz. jar roasted red peppers, drained and chopped
1/4 c. fresh basil, chopped, or 1 T. dried basil
salt and pepper to taste

Prepare tortellini according to package directions. Drain, reserving 1/4 cup cooking liquid, and return tortellini to pan. Meanwhile, melt butter and oil in a skillet over medium-high heat. Add artichokes and red peppers. Cook for 5 minutes, stirring often. Add artichoke mixture, reserved cooking liquid and basil to tortellini. Season with salt and pepper; toss to combine.

★ FREEZER FINDS ★ Keep a few packages of frozen cheese ravioli, tortellini or pierogies tucked in the freezer for easy meal-making anytime. Quickly cooked and topped with your favorite sauce, they're terrific as either a side dish or a meatless main.

Tortellini with Artichokes & Roasted Peppers

Glenna Martin, Uwchland, PA

Chicken Spaghetti

This is an old family favorite. It is a complete meal in a skillet!

Makes 4 servings

1 lb. boneless, skinless chicken
   breasts, cut into bite-size pieces
1/4 to 1/2 c. butter
1 onion, chopped
8-oz. can sliced mushrooms, drained
16-oz. pkg. frozen broccoli flowerets,
   thawed
1 clove garlic, minced
salt and pepper to taste
16-oz. pkg. spaghetti, cooked
Garnish: grated Parmesan cheese

In a large skillet, sauté chicken in butter until no longer pink. Add onion, mushrooms, broccoli and garlic; sauté until chicken is cooked through and vegetables are tender. Add salt and pepper to taste; toss with cooked spaghetti. Sprinkle with Parmesan cheese.

Kelli Venable, Ostrander, OH

Fresh Veggies & Angel Hair

My mom & I love this yummy summertime meal...just add a slice or two of garlic bread and enjoy!

Makes 2 servings

7-oz. pkg. angel hair pasta, uncooked
   and divided
1 T. olive oil
2 zucchini, peeled if desired and
   diced
2 yellow squash, diced
1 c. sliced mushrooms
1/2 c. onion, chopped
salt and pepper to taste

Divide pasta in half; reserve one-half for another recipe. Cook remaining pasta according to package directions; drain. Meanwhile, heat oil in a skillet over medium heat. Add zucchini, yellow squash, mushrooms and onion to skillet; cook until crisp-tender. Season with salt and pepper; ladle sauce over pasta.

Chicken Spaghetti

Kerry Mayer, Dunham Springs, LA

Western Pork Chops

For a delicious variation, try substituting peeled, cubed sweet potatoes for the redskins!

Makes 4 servings

1 T. all-purpose flour
1 c. barbecue sauce
4 pork chops
salt and pepper to taste
4 redskin potatoes, sliced
1 green pepper, cubed
1 c. baby carrots

Shake flour in a large plastic zipping bag. Add barbecue sauce to bag and squeeze bag to blend in flour. Season pork chops with salt and pepper; add pork chops to bag. Turn bag to coat pork chops with sauce. On a baking sheet, arrange vegetables in an even layer. Remove pork chops from bag and place on top of vegetables. Cover with aluminum foil, making a slit on the top. Bake at 350 degrees for about 40 to 45 minutes, until pork chops and vegetables are tender.

★ TIME-SAVING SHORTCUT ★ **Homemade applesauce goes so well with pork chops...why not make some while dinner is cooking? Peel, core and chop 4 tart apples. Combine with 1/4 cup water, 2 teaspoons brown sugar and 1/8 teaspoon cinnamon in a microwave-safe bowl. Cover and microwave on high for 8 to 10 minutes. Mash apples with a potato masher and serve warm, dusted with a little more cinnamon.**

Western Pork Chops

Brandi Glenn, Los Osos, CA

Gobblin' Good Turkey Burgers

This was my mom's recipe...I'll take these over plain old hamburgers any day!

Makes 4 to 6 sandwiches

1 lb. ground turkey
1 onion, minced
1 c. shredded Cheddar cheese
1/4 c. Worcestershire sauce
1/2 t. dry mustard
salt and pepper to taste
6 to 8 hamburger buns, split

Combine all ingredients except buns; form into 4 to 6 patties. Grill to desired doneness; serve on hamburger buns.

LaShelle Brown, Mulvane, KS

Idaho Tacos

This is a tasty quick & easy meal to toss together on a busy day. If time is short, you can bake the potatoes in the microwave while you are making the beef mixture.

Makes 4 servings

4 russet potatoes
1 lb. ground beef
1-1/4 oz. pkg. taco seasoning mix
1/2 c. water
1 c. shredded Cheddar cheese
Garnish: sour cream, sliced
    green onions
Optional: salsa

Pierce potatoes several times with a fork. Bake at 400 degrees for 50 to 55 minutes, until fork-tender. With a sharp knife, cut an X in the top of each warm potato; fluff pulp with a fork and set aside. Brown beef in a skillet over medium heat; drain. Stir in seasoning mix and water; bring to a boil. Simmer over low heat for 5 to 7 minutes, stirring occasionally. To serve, top potatoes with beef mixture, cheese, sour cream, onions and salsa, if desired.

Gobblin' Good Turkey Burgers

Linda Kilgore, Kittanning, PA

Deep-Dish Skillet Pizza

This recipe is my husband's. He made us one of these pizzas for supper and now it's the only pizza we ever want to eat. Delicious!

Makes 4 servings

1 loaf frozen bread dough, thawed
1 to 2 15-oz. jars pizza sauce
1/2 lb. ground pork sausage, browned
  and drained
5-oz. pkg. sliced pepperoni
1/2 c. sliced mushrooms
1/2 c. green pepper, sliced
Italian seasoning to taste
1 c. shredded mozzarella cheese
1 c. shredded Cheddar cheese

Generously grease a large cast-iron skillet. Press thawed dough into the bottom and up the sides of skillet. Spread desired amount of pizza sauce over dough. Add favorite toppings, ending with cheeses on top. Bake at 425 degrees for 30 minutes. Carefully remove skillet from oven. Let stand several minutes; pizza will finish baking in the skillet. Cut into wedges to serve.

★ MAKE IT YOURS ★ Just for fun, divide your bread dough into smaller portions and bake in individually sized cast-iron skillets. Everyone gets their own pizza!

Deep-Dish Skillet Pizza

Amanda Homan, Columbus, OH

Tarragon Steak Dinner Salad

Delicious...a perfect light summer meal.

Makes 4 servings

6 c. Boston lettuce
2 pears, peeled, cored and sliced
1/2 red onion, thinly sliced
1/2 lb. grilled beef steak, thinly
 sliced
1/4 c. crumbled blue cheese
1/2 c. red wine vinaigrette
 salad dressing
1 T. fresh tarragon, minced
1/4 t. pepper

Arrange lettuce, pears and onion on 4 serving plates. Top with sliced steak and sprinkle with cheese. Combine dressing, tarragon and pepper in a small bowl; whisk well. Drizzle dressing mixture over salad.

Tori Willis, Champaign, IL

Minted Baby Carrots

I make these carrots often...they are so easy to fix and everyone loves them!

Makes 4 servings

1/2 lb. baby carrots
1 T. butter
salt and pepper to taste
1 T. lemon zest, minced
1 T. brown sugar, packed
2 t. fresh mint, minced

In a stockpot of boiling water, cook carrots 5 minutes. Remove from heat; drain. Melt butter in a skillet over medium-high heat. Stir in carrots; cook until crisp-tender. Season with salt and pepper to taste. Combine remaining ingredients; sprinkle over individual servings.

Tarragon Steak Dinner Salad

Jennifer Williams, Los Angeles, CA

Cheeseburger Bake

This hearty meal is great after a long day of work and errands...so filling.

Makes 4 servings

8-oz. tube refrigerated crescent rolls
1 lb. ground beef
1-1/4 oz. pkg. taco seasoning mix
15-oz. can tomato sauce
2 c. shredded Cheddar cheese
Garnish: chopped green onions

Unroll crescent roll dough; separate triangles and press into a greased 9" round baking pan, pinching seams closed. Bake at 350 degrees for 10 minutes; set aside. Meanwhile, brown beef in a skillet over medium heat; drain. Add taco seasoning and sauce; heat through. Spoon over crescent rolls and sprinkle cheese on top. Bake, uncovered, for 10 to 15 minutes. Let stand 5 minutes before serving. Garnish with chopped green onions.

Dianne Young, South Jordan, UT

Beef & Cheddar Quiche

So yummy topped with sour cream or even salsa!

Makes 8 servings

3 eggs, beaten
1 c. whipping cream
1 c. shredded Cheddar cheese
1 c. ground beef, browned and drained
9-inch pie crust

Mix eggs, cream, cheese and beef together; spread into pie crust. Bake at 450 degrees for 15 minutes; lower oven temperature to 350 degrees and continue baking for 15 minutes.

★ STORE IT ★ Extra ground beef is tasty in so many easy recipes...tacos, chili and casseroles to name a few! Brown 3 or 4 pounds at a time, divide it into plastic zipping bags and refrigerate or freeze for future use.

Cheeseburger Bake

Carol Hickman, Kingsport, TN

Salmon Patties

A delicious standby...so quick to fix, and most of the ingredients are right in the cupboard.

Serves 5 to 6

15-1/2 oz. can salmon, drained and
   flaked
1/2 c. round buttery crackers,
   crushed
1/2 T. dried parsley
1/2 t. lemon zest
1 T. lemon juice
2 green onions, sliced
1 egg, beaten
2 T. oil
Optional: 5 to 6 English muffins,
   split and toasted

Combine first 7 ingredients; form into 5 to 6 patties. Heat oil in a skillet over medium heat. Cook patties 4 to 5 minutes on each side, until golden. Serve on English muffins, if desired, topped with Cucumber Sauce.

Cucumber Sauce:

1/3 c. cucumber, chopped
1/4 c. plain yogurt
1/4 c. mayonnaise
1/4 t. dried tarragon

Combine all ingredients; chill until ready to serve.

★ SUPER SAUCE ★ Stir up a dilly of a sauce for salmon patties. Whisk together 1/2 cup sour cream, one tablespoon Dijon mustard, one tablespoon lemon juice and 2 teaspoons chopped fresh dill. Chill... so simple and so good!

Salmon Patties

Ann Heavey, Bridgewater, MA

Marty's Special Burgers

Serve these zippy burgers at your next cookout...guests will rave!

Makes 4 sandwiches

1 lb. lean ground beef
1/2 c. crumbled feta or blue cheese
1/2 c. bread crumbs
1 egg, beaten
1/2 t. salt
1/4 t. pepper
4 to 6 cherry tomatoes, halved
4 hamburger buns, split

Mix together all ingredients except buns; form into 4 burger patties. Grill over high heat to desired doneness, flipping to cook on both sides. Serve on buns.

Amanda Carew, Newfoundland, Canada

Spicy Sweet Potato Fries

Change up the sides you serve by making these sweet potato fries with just a touch of spice. They'll love them!

Serves 4 to 6

2 lbs. sweet potatoes, peeled and cut
   into wedges or strips
3 T. olive oil, divided
1 t. seasoned salt
1 t. ground cumin
1/2 t. chili powder
1/2 t. pepper
Optional: ranch salad dressing

Place sweet potatoes in a plastic zipping bag. Sprinkle with 2 tablespoons oil and seasonings; toss to coat. Drizzle remaining oil over a baking sheet; place sweet potatoes in a single layer on sheet. Bake, uncovered, at 425 degrees for 25 to 35 minutes, turning halfway through cooking time, until sweet potatoes are golden. Serve with salad dressing for dipping if desired.

Marty's Special Burgers

SIMPLE SUPPERS & SIDES

Cherylann Smith, Efland, NC

Herbed Sausage Quiche

This quiche is as beautiful as it is delicious! Serve for a fancy luncheon with fresh fruit and hot tea.

Makes 8 servings

9-inch frozen pie crust, thawed
1 c. ground pork breakfast sausage, browned and drained
3 eggs, beaten
1 c. whipping cream
1 c. shredded Cheddar cheese
1 sprig fresh rosemary, chopped
1-1/2 t. Italian seasoning
1/4 t. salt
1/4 t. pepper
Garnish: fresh rosemary sprig

Bake pie crust according to package directions. In a bowl, mix together remaining ingredients except garnish; spread into crust. Bake, uncovered, at 450 degrees for about 15 minutes. Reduce heat to 350 degrees, cover with aluminum foil and bake for 10 more minutes or until set. Garnish with rosemary sprig. Cut into wedges to serve.

Sonya Labbe, Quebec, Canada

Vegetarian Mexican Pie

When we lived in Los Angeles, I started searching for Mexican dishes that my family would love. This recipe is one of them. It's easy to make, yet so much better than any fast food.

Makes 6 servings

12 6-inch corn tortillas
1 c. low-sodium black beans, drained and rinsed
1 c. low-sodium red kidney beans, drained and rinsed
4-oz. can chopped green chiles
1-1/2 c. green or red salsa
1 c. sour cream
1 c. shredded Monterey Jack cheese

Layer 4 of the tortillas in a lightly greased 8"x8" baking pan, overlapping slightly. Top tortillas with 1/2 cup black beans, 1/2 cup kidney beans, 1/4 cup chiles, 1/2 cup salsa, 1/3 cup sour cream and 1/3 cup cheese. Add 4 more tortillas; repeat layering. Top with remaining tortillas, salsa, sour cream and cheese. Bake, uncovered, at 375 degrees, until bubbly and golden, 30 to 40 minutes.

Herbed Sausage Quiche

Shay Gardner, Portland, OR

Ultimate Cheeseburger Pizza

No need to get out the cutting board...use kitchen shears to chop tomatoes while they are still in the can.

Makes 4 servings

1/2 lb. lean ground beef
1/2 t. salt
14-1/2 oz. can whole tomatoes, drained and chopped
1 t. garlic, minced
12-inch prebaked pizza crust
1-1/2 c. shredded Cheddar cheese
1/4 c. green onions, chopped

Brown beef in a skillet over medium-high heat for about 4 minutes, stirring often, until no longer pink; drain and season with salt. Remove from heat and set aside. Stir together tomatoes and garlic; spread evenly over crust. Top with beef, cheese and onions. Place crust directly on oven rack. Bake at 450 degrees for 12 to 14 minutes, until heated through and cheese is melted.

Brenda Rogers, Atwood, CA

South-of-the-Border Squash Skillet

Our family grows lots of yellow summer squash in our community garden. We love tacos, so this taco-flavored recipe is a yummy way to use it up! If you omit the meat, it's also a great vegetarian dish.

Makes 4 servings

1 lb. ground beef or turkey
1/3 c. onion, diced
1 c. water
1-1/4 oz. pkg. taco seasoning mix
4 to 5 yellow squash, zucchini or crookneck squash, chopped
1 c. shredded Cheddar cheese

In a skillet over medium heat, brown meat with onion; drain. Stir in water and taco seasoning; add squash. Cover and simmer for about 10 minutes, until squash is tender. Stir in cheese; cover and let stand just until cheese melts.

Ultimate Cheeseburger Pizza

Cheri Maxwell, Gulf Breeze, FL

Broccoli Quiche Peppers

We love these colorful peppers for a dinner that's just a little different.

Makes 4 servings

4 red, yellow or green peppers, tops
   cut off and reserved
4 eggs, beaten
1/2 c. milk
1 c. broccoli, finely chopped
1/2 t. garlic powder
1/4 t. Italian seasoning
Optional: shredded mozzarella
   cheese

Finely dice reserved tops of peppers; set aside. Place pepper shells upright in custard cups; set cups in a 9"x9" baking pan. In a bowl, whisk together eggs, milk, broccoli, diced pepper and seasonings; pour evenly into peppers. Bake, uncovered, at 325 degrees for 40 to 50 minutes, until peppers are tender and egg mixture is set. Top with cheese if desired and bake 10 more minutes. Let stand 5 minutes before serving.

Janet Bowlin, Fayetteville, AR

Country-Style Cabbage

Tossed with bacon and onion, this cabbage side is one tasty way to enjoy your daily dose of veggies!

Makes 6 servings

4 slices bacon, cut into 1/4-inch
   pieces
1/4 c. onion, thinly sliced
1 head cabbage, coarsely shredded
2 T. sugar
1/4 c. oil, divided
salt and pepper to taste

In a skillet over medium-high heat, cook bacon until crisp. Add onion and cook 2 minutes longer. Stir in cabbage and sugar. Add oil, one tablespoon at a time, as needed. Cook until cabbage begins to wilt, but is not completely soft. Serve immediately.

★ QUICK & DELICIOUS ★ **Super-speedy stuffed peppers! Just fill hollowed-out bell peppers with leftover 3-Cheese Ziti or other pasta in sauce, top with shredded cheese and bake until golden and bubbly.**

Broccoli Quiche Peppers

**Recipe and Photo Courtesy of
BeefItsWhatsForDinner.com**

Beefy Harvest Soup

Other pasta shapes, such as rotini, bowties, medium shells or ditalini, may be substituted for large elbow macaroni; adjust cooking time as needed.

Makes 5 servings

1 lb. lean ground beef
2 c. water
14-1/2 oz. can Italian-style stewed
  tomatoes
1-1/2 c. frozen mixed vegetables
4 c. reduced-sodium beef broth
1 c. large elbow macaroni, uncooked
1/4 lb. smoked beef sausage, sliced
salt and pepper to taste

Heat a large non-stick skillet over medium heat until hot. Add beef; cook 8 to 10 minutes, breaking into crumbles and stirring occasionally. Remove from skillet with a slotted spoon. Remove drippings. Meanwhile, combine water, tomatoes with juice, vegetables and broth in a large saucepan; bring to a boil. Stir in macaroni and beef; return to a boil. Reduce heat; simmer, uncovered, 8 minutes, stirring occasionally. Stir in sausage; continue simmering 2 to 4 minutes, or until macaroni is tender and beef sausage is cooked through. Season with salt and pepper, as desired.

★ HANDY TOOLS ★ Kitchen shears are so handy for cutting stewed tomatoes right in the can, snipping fresh herbs, and snipping the ends off fresh green beans. Just remember to wash them with soap and water after each use.

Beefy Harvest Soup

Stacie Avner, Delaware, OH

Dijon Chicken & Fresh Herbs

I love making this family favorite in the summertime with my fresh garden herbs.

Makes 6 servings

6 boneless, skinless chicken breasts
1/2 t. kosher salt
1 t. pepper
3 to 4 T. Dijon mustard
2 T. fresh rosemary, minced
2 T. fresh thyme, minced
2 T. fresh parsley, minced

Sprinkle chicken with salt and pepper. Grill over medium-high heat 6 minutes per side, or until juices run clear. Remove from grill and brush both sides with mustard; sprinkle with herbs.

Amy Butcher, Columbus, GA

Garlicky Baked Shrimp

Here's the perfect party recipe... guests peel their own shrimp and save you the work!

Makes 6 servings

2 lbs. uncooked large shrimp, cleaned and unpeeled
16-oz. bottle light Italian salad dressing
1-1/2 T. pepper
2 cloves garlic, pressed
2 lemons, halved
1/4 c. fresh parsley, chopped
2 T. butter, cut into small pieces

Place shrimp, salad dressing, pepper and garlic in an ungreased 13"x9" baking pan, tossing to coat. Squeeze juice from lemons over shrimp mixture; stir. Cut lemon halves into wedges and add to pan. Sprinkle shrimp with parsley; dot with butter. Bake, uncovered, at 375 degrees for 25 minutes, stirring after 15 minutes. Serve in pan.

Dijon Chicken & Fresh Herbs

Cris Goode, Mooresville, IN

Good & Healthy "Fried" Chicken

We love this healthier version of everyone's favorite food... fried chicken!

Makes 5 servings

1 c. whole-grain panko bread crumbs
1 c. cornmeal
2 T. all-purpose flour
salt and pepper to taste
1 c. buttermilk
10 chicken drumsticks

Combine panko, cornmeal, flour, salt and pepper in a gallon-size plastic zipping bag. Coat chicken with buttermilk, one piece at a time. Drop chicken into bag and shake to coat pieces lightly. Arrange chicken in one to two 13"x9" baking pans coated with non-stick vegetable spray. Bake, uncovered, at 350 degrees for 40 to 50 minutes, until chicken juices run clear.

Michelle Powell, Valley, AL

Comforting Creamed Corn

This recipe is perfect when we are in the mood for some real comfort food!

Makes 8 servings

1 T. butter
4 c. corn, thawed if frozen
1/2 c. plain Greek yogurt
2 T. grated Parmesan cheese
1 t. dried basil

Melt butter in a non-stick skillet over medium heat; add corn. Cook for about 6 minutes, stirring occasionally, until tender. Reduce heat; stir in yogurt and cook for 4 minutes. Stir in cheese and basil just before serving.

Good & Healthy "Fried" Chicken

Judy Davis, Muskogee, OK

Mushroom-Garlic-Chicken Pizza

This recipe gets a big "YUM" at our house...try it! It's a great way to use leftover baked or grilled chicken too.

Serves 6 to 8

12-inch Italian pizza crust
3/4 c. ranch salad dressing
2 T. garlic, minced
1 chicken breast, cooked and sliced
2 4-oz. cans sliced mushrooms, drained
salt and pepper to taste
8-oz. pkg. shredded mozzarella cheese
Optional: fresh oregano leaves, red pepper flakes

Place crust on an ungreased pizza pan or baking sheet. Spread salad dressing and garlic over crust. Arrange sliced chicken and mushrooms on top. Add salt and pepper to taste; cover with cheese. Bake at 400 degrees for 8 to 10 minutes, until cheese melts. Cut into wedges. Garnish with oregano and red pepper, if desired.

Deborah Lomax, Peoria, IL

Raspberry-Dijon Baguettes

A friend shared a similar recipe using roast beef...this is my spin on that recipe using grilled chicken.

Makes 4 servings

1 baguette, sliced
1 T. Dijon mustard
1 T. raspberry jam
4 boneless, skinless chicken breasts, grilled and sliced
2 c. arugula leaves
Optional: red onion slices

Spread 4 slices of baguette with mustard. Top remaining slices with raspberry jam. Arrange a layer of grilled chicken over mustard; top with arugula and onion, if desired. Top with remaining baguette slices.

Mushroom-Garlic-Chicken Pizza

Raspberry Yogurt Muffins, Page 186

CHAPTER FIVE

Quick Breads, Biscuits, Rolls & Muffins

Easy Banana Bread, Page 206

Quick Strawberry Cream Danish, Page 188

Brenda Huey, Geneva, IN

Dreamy Orange Muffins

I love these muffins! They are moist and oh-so good. I make these for sale in my Cobblestone Bakery and they're a favorite.

Makes one dozen

8-oz. container orange-flavored
  yogurt
1 c. buttermilk
1-1/2 c. orange juice, divided
3 eggs, beaten
1 c. margarine, softened
1-1/2 c. sugar
2 T. baking powder
4 c. all-purpose flour
11-oz. can mandarin oranges,
  drained
2 c. powdered sugar

In a large bowl, combine yogurt, buttermilk, one cup orange juice, eggs, margarine and sugar. Stir until combined. Add baking powder and flour; mix just until combined. Stir in oranges. Grease a 12-cup muffin tin or line with paper liners. Fill muffin cups 2/3 full. Bake at 325 degrees for 20 to 25 minutes, or until a toothpick inserted in the center tests clean. Mix remaining orange juice with powdered sugar; drizzle over cooled muffins.

★ DID YOU KNOW? ★ You won't need a pastry bag to drizzle icing over these Dreamy Orange Muffins. You can simply use a teaspoon, or fill a plastic zipping bag with icing, seal the bag shut and make a snip on the bottom corner!

Dreamy Orange Muffins

Karen Crooks, West Des Moines, IA

Nutmeg Crunch Coffee Cake

A sweet neighbor shared this recipe with me over 25 years ago and I've never seen a similar one. It's simple, but fantastic...the topping bakes into wonderful deep crevices of brown sugar infused with nutmeg. You must try it!

Serves 10 to 12

2 c. all-purpose flour
1 t. baking powder
1 t. baking soda
1/2 t. salt
1/2 t. cinnamon
2/3 c. butter, softened
1 c. sugar
1/2 c. brown sugar, packed
2 eggs, beaten
1 c. buttermilk

In a bowl, mix flour, baking powder, baking soda, salt and cinnamon; set aside. In a large bowl, blend butter and sugars until light and fluffy, about 2 to 3 minutes. Add eggs, one at a time; mix until well blended. Add flour mixture to butter mixture alternately with buttermilk, beginning and ending with flour mixture. Stir well. Pour batter into a 13"x9" baking pan sprayed with non-stick vegetable spray. Sprinkle Brown Sugar Topping over batter. Bake at 350 degrees for about 30 minutes.

Brown Sugar Topping:

1/2 c. brown sugar, packed
1/2 t. cinnamon
1/4 to 1/2 t. nutmeg

Mix all ingredients in a small bowl.

★ SIMPLY SPICED ★ Serve hot spiced coffee with fresh-baked coffee cake. Simply add 3/4 teaspoon apple pie spice to 1/2 cup ground coffee and brew as usual.

Nutmeg Crunch Coffee Cake

Brenda Trnka, Manitoba, Canada

Quick Poppy Seed Muffins

Such an easy recipe! These are terrific at breakfast, with tea or for after-school snacks.

Makes 2 dozen

18-1/4 oz. pkg. lemon cake mix
 with pudding
1/2 c. poppy seed
Optional: favorite jam

Prepare cake batter according to package directions. Add poppy seed; mix well. Fill greased muffin cups 2/3 full. Top each muffin with a sprinkle of sugar. Bake at 350 degrees for about 8 to 10 minutes, until muffins test done. Top with a dollop of jam, if desired.

Holly Curry, Middleburgh, NY

Poppy Seed Cake

The glaze drizzled over this simple cake sets it apart from other poppy seed cakes.

Serves 8 to 10

18-1/4 oz. pkg. yellow cake mix
1 c. oil
1 c. sour cream
1/2 c. sugar
4 eggs, beaten
1/4 c. poppy seed

In a large bowl, beat together dry cake mix and all remaining ingredients. Pour into a greased and floured Bundt® pan. Bake at 325 degrees for one hour, or until a toothpick inserted near the center tests clean. Turn cake out onto a serving plate. Drizzle Glaze over top.

Glaze:

1/2 c. sugar
1/4 c. orange juice
1/2 t. almond extract
1/2 t. imitation butter flavor
1/2 t. vanilla extract

Combine all ingredients; mix well.

Quick Poppy Seed Muffins

Beth Bundy, Long Prairie, MN

Raspberry Yogurt Muffins

I came across this recipe in an old farmers' cookbook. I'm so happy I did, they are delicious!

Makes 2 dozen

1 c. quick-cooking oats,
  uncooked
1/2 c. brown sugar, packed
1 c. vanilla or plain yogurt
1/2 c. oil
1 egg, beaten
1 c. all-purpose flour
1 t. salt
1 t. baking powder
1/2 t. baking soda
1 c. raspberries or other fruit,
  finely chopped

In a bowl, combine oats, brown sugar, yogurt, oil and egg. Beat well; let stand 5 minutes. Sift in flour, salt, baking power and baking soda. Before stirring, sprinkle fruit over flour mixture. Stir to blend. Fill greased muffin cups 2/3 full. Bake at 400 degrees for 20 minutes.

Dawn Schlauderaff, Brooklyn Park, MN

Quickie Cornbread

A friend at work shared this 2-ingredient wonder with me.

Makes 8 servings

8-1/2 oz. pkg. corn muffin mix
14-3/4 oz. can creamed corn

In a bowl, stir together corn muffin mix and creamed corn until moistened. Pour batter into an 8"x8" baking pan sprayed with non-stick vegetable spray. Bake at 400 degrees for 20 to 25 minutes, until set and golden. Cut into squares.

★ FREEZE IT ★ Serve up freshly baked muffins any time! Place muffins in a freezer bag and freeze. To warm frozen muffins, wrap in heavy foil and pop into a 300-degree oven for 12 to 15 minutes.

Raspberry Yogurt Muffins

Beth Bundy, Long Prairie, MN

Quick Strawberry Cream Danish

These are super easy, super tasty and super pretty. A couple of these with your coffee will definitely make your morning bright!

Makes 16 servings

2 8-oz. pkgs. cream cheese, softened
1 egg, separated
1 t. vanilla extract
1 t. lemon juice
1 T. all-purpose flour
2 8-oz. tubes refrigerated crescent rolls
1/2 c. strawberry preserves, divided

Beat together cream cheese, egg yolk, vanilla, lemon juice and flour. Unroll and separate rolls; place a teaspoon of cream cheese mixture in the center of each triangle. Fold over edges of rolls, leaving center open. Brush with beaten egg white. Place on ungreased baking sheets. Bake at 350 degrees for 20 minutes. Remove from oven and cool slightly. Top each with a teaspoon of strawberry preserves.

Kathy Grashoff, Fort Wayne, IN

Blueberry Buckle Coffee Cake

Fresh blueberries are a summertime treat to be savored and we love them. This coffee cake showcases them well!

Makes 9 servings

2 c. all-purpose flour
3/4 c. sugar
2-1/2 t. baking powder
3/4 t. salt
1/4 c. butter
3/4 c. 2% milk
2 c. blueberries

Mix together all ingredients except berries. Beat for 30 seconds; carefully fold in berries. Spread batter into a greased 9"x9" baking pan; sprinkle with Crumb Topping. Bake at 375 degrees for 45 to 50 minutes.

Crumb Topping:

1/4 c. brown sugar, packed
1/3 c. all-purpose flour
3 T. butter, softened
1/2 t. cinnamon

Mix all ingredients together until crumbly.

Quick Strawberry Cream Danish

Hope Davenport, Portland, TX

Pecan Bites

These sweet morsels don't even need any frosting!

Makes about 1-1/2 dozen

1 c. brown sugar, packed
1/2 c. all-purpose flour
1 c. chopped pecans
2/3 c. butter, melted and cooled
  slightly
2 eggs, beaten

Combine sugar, flour and pecans in a large bowl; set aside. In a separate bowl, whisk together together butter and eggs; stir into flour mixture. Spoon batter into greased and floured mini muffin cups, filling 2/3 full. Bake at 350 degrees for 22 to 25 minutes, until golden. Cool on a wire rack.

Mertie Stardevant, Washington, NC

Beer Bread Biscuits

This simple recipe is from my sister-in-law. It's a hit every time we have soup!

Makes 6 to 8 biscuits

2 c. biscuit baking mix
3 T. sugar
12-oz. can regular or non-alcoholic
  beer

Combine all ingredients in a bowl; mix well. Spoon batter into greased muffin cups, filling 3/4 full. Bake at 325 degrees for 20 minutes.

★ MAKE IT YOURSELF ★ Next time a recipe call for toasted nuts or coconut, toast your own. Spread chopped nuts or flaked coconut in a shallow pan and bake at 350 degrees for 7 to 12 minutes, stirring often until golden.

Pecan Bites

Rita Morgan, Pueblo, CO

Herbed Cheese Focaccia

This savory bread is a favorite, scrumptious for snacking or to accompany a tossed salad.

Serves 12 to 14

13.8-oz. tube refrigerated pizza
  dough
1 onion, finely chopped
2 cloves garlic, minced
2 T. olive oil
1 t. dried basil
1 t. dried oregano
1/2 t. dried rosemary
1 c. shredded mozzarella cheese

Unroll dough on a greased baking sheet. Press with fingers to form indentations; set aside. Sauté onion and garlic in oil in a skillet; remove from heat. Stir in herbs; spread mixture evenly over dough. Sprinkle with cheese. Bake at 400 degrees for 10 to 15 minutes, until golden.

Sharon Crider, Junction City, KS

Parmesan Supper Bread

With this recipe, it's oh-so easy to serve freshly baked bread at dinnertime.

Serves 6 to 8

1-1/2 c. buttermilk baking mix
1 T. sugar
1 T. dried minced onion
1/2 t. dried oregano
1 egg, beaten
1/4 c. milk
1/4 c. water
1/4 c. grated Parmesan cheese

In a bowl, combine all ingredients except cheese. Mix with a fork until soft dough forms. Spread dough in a greased 8" round cake pan; sprinkle with cheese. Bake at 400 degrees for 20 to 25 minutes, until golden. Cut into wedges and serve warm.

★ VARIETY FOR FUN ★ Offer a variety of breads when sharing your favorite fondue. Herbed Cheese Focaccia is a delightful choice, along with rosemary-garlic, tomato-basil, sourdough, ciabatta and sesame, all with unique flavors...you just might discover a new favorite.

Herbed Cheese Focaccia

Dobie Hill, Lubbock, TX

Buttermilk Cinnamon Rolls

These no-yeast rolls are super easy and fast to make and are always a treat!

Makes 15 servings

3 c. all-purpose flour
4 t. baking powder
1/4 t. baking soda
1 t. salt
1/2 c. cold butter
1-1/2 c. buttermilk
1/4 c. butter, softened
1/2 c. sugar
1 t. cinnamon

In a large bowl, combine flour, baking powder, baking soda and salt; cut in cold butter until crumbs form. Stir in buttermilk until well blended; knead dough on a lightly floured surface for 4 to 5 minutes. Roll out to 1/4-inch thickness; spread softened butter over dough to edges. In a small bowl, mix sugar and cinnamon; sprinkle over dough. Roll up jelly-roll style; cut into 1/2-inch slices. Place on 2 greased baking sheets; bake at 400 degrees for 10 to 12 minutes.

★ DOUBLE DUTY ★ Tuck odds & ends of leftover cinnamon rolls, fruit muffins and doughnuts into a freezer container...they're scrumptious in your favorite bread pudding recipe.

Buttermilk Cinnamon Rolls

Rita Morgan, Pueblo, CO

Southwestern Flatbread

Yum...hot fresh-baked bread to enjoy for breakfast with a cup of fresh fruit! Easy to change up to Italian flavors too, with oregano and Parmesan cheese.

Makes about 15 pieces

2 t. olive oil, divided
11-oz. tube refrigerated crusty
  French loaf
1/2 c. roasted sunflower kernels
1 t. chili powder
1/2 to 1 t. coarse salt

Brush a 15"x10" sheet pan with one teaspoon oil; unroll dough onto pan. Use a floured rolling pin to roll out into a rectangle. Drizzle dough with remaining oil; brush over dough. In a small bowl, combine sunflower kernels and chili powder; mix well and sprinkle over the dough. Firmly press sunflower kernels into dough; sprinkle top with salt. Bake at 375 degrees for 12 to 16 minutes, until golden. Remove flatbread to a wire rack; cool 10 minutes. Tear or cut into pieces..

★ SAVVY SWAP ★ Put a new spin on sandwiches by swapping out the same ol' buns with different types of bread like Southwestern Flatbread, English muffins, Italian ciabatta or sliced French bread. Pita rounds make sandwiches that are easier for littler hands to hold.

Southwestern Flatbread

Lisa Gibbs, Nashville, TN

Speedy Sausage Muffins

My mother-in-law bakes these muffins for us. She serves them with hot coffee and spiced tea...so nice on a cool morning!

Makes 16 muffins

1 lb. ground pork sausage,
  browned and drained
3 c. biscuit baking mix
1-1/2 c. shredded Cheddar
  cheese
10-3/4 oz. can Cheddar cheese
  soup
3/4 c. water

Combine sausage, baking mix and cheese in a large bowl; make a well in center of mixture. Stir together soup and water; add to sausage mixture, stirring just until combined. Spoon into lightly greased muffin cups, filling to top of cups. Bake at 375 degrees for 20 to 25 minutes, until lightly golden.

Kerry Mayer, Dunham Springs, LA

Quick Cheese Biscuits

At my house, hot bread is a must at dinnertime. This recipe is so easy that my daughter often helps.

Makes 1-1/2 dozen

2 c. biscuit baking mix
2/3 c. milk
2/3 c. shredded Cheddar cheese
1/4 c. butter, melted
1 t. garlic powder

In a bowl, combine baking mix, milk and cheese; mix well. Drop batter by heaping tablespoonfuls onto a lightly greased baking sheet. Bake at 450 degrees for 8 to 10 minutes. Combine butter and garlic powder; brush over hot biscuits when they come out of the oven.

★ IN A PINCH ★ Out of biscuit baking mix? No problem! For each cup needed in a recipe, use 1 cup all-purpose flour, 1-1/2 teaspoons baking powder, 1/2 teaspoon salt and 1 tablespoon shortening.

Speedy Sausage Muffins

Vickie, Gooseberry Patch

Sweet Potato Cornbread

This rich cornbread is sure to become your family favorite. Baking it in a skillet makes the edges so wonderfully golden brown. Serve it with honey butter or raspberry jam.

Makes 6 servings

2 c. self-rising cornmeal mix
1/4 c. sugar
1 t. cinnamon
1-1/2 c. milk
1 c. cooked sweet potato, mashed
1/4 c. butter, melted
1 egg, beaten

Whisk together all ingredients just until dry ingredients are moistened. Spoon batter into a greased 8" cast-iron skillet or pan. Bake at 425 degrees for 30 minutes or until a toothpick inserted in center comes out clean.

Dan Needham, Columbus, OH

Swope Bread

My grandmother used to make this simple batter bread. We never did find out where the name came from, but it is tasty and easy to make. Serve with a favorite chicken salad.

Makes one loaf

2 c. whole-wheat flour
1 c. all-purpose flour
1/2 c. sugar
1 t. salt
2 t. baking soda
2 c. buttermilk
Optional: 3/4 c. raisins

In a large bowl, stir together flours, sugar and salt; set aside. In a separate bowl, dissolve baking soda in buttermilk. Stir buttermilk mixture into flour mixture; beat well. Fold in raisins, if desired. Pour batter into a lightly greased 9"x5" loaf pan. Bake at 350 degrees for one hour, until golden. Cool on a wire rack.

Sweet Potato Cornbread

Sonna Johnson, Goldfield, IA

Cranberry Applesauce Muffins

I like to make these by the dozen and take them to church for after-church coffee.

Makes 2 dozen

1 c. fresh or frozen cranberries
1-1/4 c. unsweetened applesauce
1/3 c. canola oil
1 egg, beaten
2 c. all-purpose flour
1/2 c. sugar
1 t. baking soda
1 t. cinnamon
1/2 t. salt

Using a food processor, process cranberries until chopped. Set aside. In a small bowl, mix applesauce, oil and egg. In a large bowl, combine flour, sugar, baking soda, cinnamon and salt. Make a well in the flour mixture. Slowly pour in applesauce mixture, stirring until just moistened. Fold in cranberries. Fill 24 greased or paper-lined muffin cups 2/3 full. Bake at 350 degrees for 25 to 30 minutes, until a wooden toothpick inserted in the center comes out clean. Cool for 2 minutes before removing from cups.

★ TASTY MIX ★ Pair a basket of warm Cranberry Applesauce Muffins with a crock of fruit butter...yum! Simply blend 1/2 cup each of softened butter and strawberry, apricot or peach preserves.

Cranberry Applesauce Muffins

Lisa Ashton, Aston, PA

Chocolate Pinwheels

We love to serve these yummy treats with warm spiced milk... the perfect combination!

Makes 16 servings

11-oz. tube refrigerated bread
  sticks
3/4 c. semi-sweet chocolate chips
1/4 c. butter, melted
1/2 c. sugar

Unroll bread sticks and cut them in half. Press chocolate chips in a single row along the top of each bread stick half; roll up into a pinwheel shape. Arrange pinwheels on a parchment paper-lined baking sheet. Brush with melted butter; sprinle with sugar. Bake at 350 degrees for 10 to 12 minutes, until golden.

Jody Pressley, Charlotte, NC

Bran & Raisin Muffins

These bran muffins are an all-time favorite with just about everyone!

Makes one dozen

2 c. bran & raisin cereal
1-1/2 c. skim milk
1-1/2 c. all-purpose flour
1 t. baking soda
1/4 t. salt
1 egg, beaten
1/2 c. brown sugar, packed
2 T. butter, melted

Mix cereal with milk; set aside. In a large bowl, combine remaining ingredients; stir in cereal mixture. Fill lightly greased or paper-lined muffin cups about 2/3 full with batter. Bake at 350 degrees for 20 to 25 minutes.

★ JUICY TIP ★ For plump, juicy raisins or dried cranberries, cover them with boiling water and let stand for 15 minutes. Drain and pat dry with a paper towel before adding to a muffin recipe.

Chocolate Pinwheels

Noah Burnley, Ankeny, IA

Easy Banana Bread

This recipe is a staple at our house!

Makes 10 servings

3 ripe bananas, peeled
1 c. sugar
1/2 c. butter, softened
2 eggs
2 c. all-purpose flour
3 T. buttermilk
1 t. baking powder
1 t. baking soda
1/2 t. salt

Using a fork, mash the bananas until softened. Set aside. In a large mixing bowl, combine sugar and butter. Beat until creamy. Add eggs and mashed bananas; mix well. In a small bowl, mix flour, buttermilk, baking powder, baking soda and salt. Add to butter mixture and mix well. Add flour mixture to butter mixture and mix well. Pour into a greased 9"x5" loaf pan. Bake at 350 degrees for about 40 minutes, or when a toothpick comes out clean when inserted in the center.

Mary Patenaude, Griswold, CT

Fresh Strawberry Bread

Serve this delicious bread with a dab of homemade strawberry jam or cream cheese.

Makes 2 loaves

3 c. all-purpose flour
2 c. sugar
1-1/2 t. cinnamon
1 t. baking soda
1 t. salt
4 eggs, beaten
1 c. oil
2 c. strawberries, hulled and diced
Optional: 1-1/4 c. chopped nuts

In a bowl, combine flour, sugar, cinnamon, baking soda and salt. In a separate bowl, whisk together eggs and oil; fold in strawberries. Gradually add egg mixture to flour mixture; stir until just moistened. Add nuts, if using. Pour batter into 2 greased and floured 9"x5" loaf pans. Bake at 350 degrees for one hour.

Easy Banana Bread

Trisha Donley, Pinedale, WY

Cheese & Basil Scones

I love to serve these scones with hearty soups.

Makes one dozen

2 c. all-purpose flour
1/4 c. shredded Parmesan or
   Romano cheese
2 t. baking powder
1 t. baking soda
2 T. fresh basil, chopped
1/4 t. pepper
2/3 c. buttermilk
3 T. olive oil
Optional: 1 egg, beaten

In a bowl, combine flour, cheese, baking powder, baking soda, basil and pepper. Add buttermilk and oil; stir just until moistened. Knead gently 3 times on a floured surface. Line baking sheet with parchment paper. On lined baking sheet, pat dough into a rectangle; cut into 12 squares. Pull apart slightly. If desired, brush dough with egg to glaze. Bake at 450 degrees for 10 to 12 minutes, until golden. Serve warm or at room temperature.

Darlene Fuller, Greenville, KY

Cheddar & Green Pepper Cornbread

One of our favorite comfort foods is cornbread. This dressed-up version is our favorite!

Serves 10 to 12

1 c. self-rising flour
1 c. cornmeal
1/4 t. onion salt
1 egg, beaten
1-1/2 c. milk
1 c. corn
1/2 c. green pepper, chopped
1 c. shredded Cheddar cheese

Combine flour, cornmeal, onion salt, egg and milk in a large bowl; stir until moistened. Stir in remaining ingredients; mix well. Spread in a lightly greased 13"x9" baking pan. Bake at 375 degrees for 30 minutes, or until golden.,

Cheese & Basil Scones

Kelly Marshall, Olathe, KS

Kelly's Easy Caramel Rolls

This is a much-requested family recipe! Serve with a fruit salad for a special brunch.

Makes 10 rolls

3 T. corn syrup, divided
3 T. brown sugar, packed and divided
3 T. chopped pecans, divided
2 T. butter, cubed and divided
12-oz. tube refrigerated biscuits

To each of 10 greased muffin cups, add one teaspoon each of syrup, brown sugar and pecans. Top each with 1/2 teaspoon butter and one biscuit. Bake at 400 degrees for 8 to 10 minutes, until golden. Invert rolls onto a plate before serving.

Janis Parr, Ontario, Canada

Cinnamon Sensation Bread

This is a delicious breakfast bread, rich, spicy and oh-so good!

Makes 6 servings

2 T. butter, softened
1-1/2 c. sugar
1 egg, beaten
2 c. all-purpose flour
2 t. baking powder
1/4 t. salt
1 c. milk

In a large bowl, blend butter and sugar; stir in egg. Add flour, baking powder and salt alternately with milk; mix well. Pour batter into a greased 8"x8" baking pan; sprinkle with Cinnamon Topping. Bake at 375 degrees for 30 to 35 minutes, until a toothpick inserted in the center tests clean. Cut into squares; serve warm.

Cinnamon Topping:

1 c. brown sugar, packed
1/4 c. butter, softened
3/4 t. cinnamon

In a bowl, work together butter and brown sugar with your fingertips until well mixed. Stir in cinnamon.

Kelly's Easy Caramel Rolls

Lynn Williams, Muncie, IN

Soft Sesame Bread Sticks

These yummy bread sticks go great with soups or salads...I make plenty because they disappear quickly!

Makes one dozen

1-1/4 c. all-purpose flour
2 t. sugar
1-1/2 t. baking powder
1/2 t. salt
2/3 c. milk
2 T. butter, melted
2 t. sesame seed

In a small bowl, combine flour, sugar, baking powder and salt. Gradually add milk; stir to form a soft dough. Turn onto a floured surface; knead gently 3 to 4 times. Roll into a 10-inch by 5 1/2-inch rectangle; cut into 12 bread sticks. Place butter in a 13"x9" baking pan; coat bread sticks in butter and sprinkle with sesame seed. Bake at 450 degrees for 14 to 18 minutes, until golden.

Kym Cicero, Bristow, VA

Scrumptious Olive Bread

The men in the family ask for this all the time! A favorite at potluck suppers and parties, this bread is great as an hors d'oeuvre and deliciously complements any pasta dish. It freezes well and reheats easily in the microwave.

Makes about 16 servings

1 to 1-1/2 4-oz. jars green olives,
    drained and well minced
1/2 c. mayonnaise
1/2 c. butter, melted
8-oz. pkg. shredded Monterey Jack
    cheese
1 large wide loaf French bread, sliced
    in half lengthwise

Mix olives, mayonnaise, butter and cheese in a large bowl, blending well. Spread mixture over cut sides of bread; place on a baking sheet. Bake, uncovered, at 350 degrees for 15 minutes, or until golden and cheese is melted. Slice and serve warm.

Soft Sesame Bread Sticks

Jeanne Barringer, Edgewater, FL

Sour Cream Mini Biscuits

This recipe makes several dozen bite-size biscuits...ideal for filling gift baskets or taking to a potluck.

Makes 4 dozen

1 c. butter, softened
1 c. sour cream
2 c. self-rising flour

Blend butter and sour cream together until fluffy; gradually mix in flour. Drop teaspoonfuls of dough into greased mini muffin cups. Bake at 450 degrees for 10 to 12 minutes.

Maria Temple, New York, NY

Sugar-Topped Muffins

Enjoy these warm muffins for a real treat!

Makes 2 dozen

18-1/4 oz. pkg. white cake mix
1 c. milk
2 eggs
1/2 t. nutmeg
1/3 c. sugar
1/2 t. cinnamon
1/4 c. butter, melted

Beat cake mix, milk, eggs and nutmeg at low speed with an electric mixer until just moistened; beat at high speed 2 minutes. Fill paper-lined muffin cups 2/3 full. Bake at 350 degrees until golden, about 15 to 18 minutes. Cool 5 minutes. Combine sugar and cinnamon on a small plate. Brush muffin tops with butter; roll in sugar and cinnamon mixture. Serve warm.

★ TIME SAVER ★ Scrumptious in seconds... top Sour Cream Mini Biscuits with a small slice of deli chicken, a teaspoon of ham salad, or even top them with a dollop of scrambled egg!

Sour Cream Mini Biscuits

Leslie Williams, Americus, GA

Maple-Pecan Brunch Ring

A sweet & simple way to make a tasty treat for holiday guests.

Makes about 12 servings

3/4 c. chopped pecans
1/2 c. brown sugar, packed
2 t. cinnamon
2 17.3-oz. tubes refrigerated jumbo
   flaky biscuits
2 T. butter, melted
1/2 c. maple syrup

Combine pecans, brown sugar and cinnamon; set aside. Split each biscuit horizontally; brush half of the biscuits with butter and sprinkle with half the pecan mixture. Arrange topped biscuits in a circle on an ungreased baking sheet; overlap each biscuit slightly and keep within 2 inches of the edge of the baking sheet. Brush remaining biscuit halves with butter; sprinkle with remaining pecan mixture. Arrange a second ring just inside the first ring, overlapping edges. Bake at 350 degrees for 30 to 35 minutes, until golden. Remove to wire rack; cool 10 minutes. Brush with maple syrup.

★ SAVE FOR LATER ★ Stock up on refrigerated biscuits for fresh-baked bread anytime! Try dressing them up with herbs and garlic powder or even flatten for tasty mini pizzas.

Maple-Pecan Brunch Ring

Harvest Apple Parfait Crunch, Page 222

CHAPTER SIX

Super Easy & Delicious Desserts

Luscious Strawberry Pie, Page 236

Peanut Butter-Chocolate Bars, Page 238

DELICIOUS DESSERTS

Rebecca Etling, Blairsville, PA

Nut Macaroons

One of my favorite quick & easy cookie recipes.

Makes 2 dozen

2/3 c. sweetened condensed milk
1 c. sweetened flaked coconut
1 c. chopped nuts
1 t. vanilla extract
3/4 t. almond extract

In a bowl, mix all ingredients in the order given. Drop by teaspoonfuls onto well greased baking sheets. Bake at 350 degrees for 10 to 12 minutes, until dry around the edges.

Charlene Smith, Lombard, IL

Coconut Clouds

For extra sparkle, top with a candied cherry and sprinkle with sugar before baking.

Serves 15 to 20

2 egg whites, beaten
3/4 c. sugar
2-1/2 c. flaked coconut
1 t. vanilla extract
1/8 t. salt

Combine all ingredients together. Beat with an electric mixer on medium-high speed until soft peaks form. Drop by tablespoonfuls, one inch apart, on a greased baking sheet; bake at 350 degrees for 15 to 20 minutes. Cool on a wire rack. Store in an airtight container.

★ DID YOU KNOW? ★ Evaporated milk and sweetened condensed milk were both old standbys in Grandma's day. They're still handy today, but while they're both shelf-stable whole milk, they're not interchangeable. Condensed milk contains sugar and is cooked down to a thickened consistency, while evaporated milk contains no added sugar.

Nut Macaroons

Shirl Parsons, Cape Carteret, NC

Harvest Apple Parfait Crunch

Enjoy the flavor of fresh caramel apples in a layered dessert. It only looks like it took a lot of effort!

Makes 6 servings

8-oz. pkg. Neufchâtel cheese, softened
3/4 c. dark brown sugar, packed and divided
1 T. milk
1/2 c. granola cereal nuggets
3/4 c. dry-roasted peanuts, finely chopped
3 T. margarine, melted
4 red apples, cored and chopped
Garnish: whipped topping

Mix Neufchâtel cheese, 1/2 cup brown sugar and milk in a bowl until well blended; set aside. In a separate small bowl, combine cereal, peanuts and remaining brown sugar; stir in melted margarine until well blended. Spoon half of the apples into 6 parfait glasses; cover with half each of cheese mixture and cereal mixture. Add a dollop of whipped topping. Repeat layering, ending with topping. Serve immediately, or cover and chill.

★ FRESH-PICKED ★ Head out to a pick-your-own apple orchard for a day of fresh-air fun. The kids will love it, and you'll come home with bushels of the best-tasting apples for parfaits, applesauce, cobblers and crisps!

Harvest Apple Parfait Crunch

MaryAlice Dobbert, King George, VA

Caramel Apple Pie Dump Cake

This recipe takes about five minutes to put together! Great fall flavors and aromas will warm your kitchen.

Serves 8 to 10

2 21-oz. cans apple pie filling
1/4 c. caramel ice cream topping
18-1/2 oz. pkg. yellow cake mix
1/2 c. butter, melted
Garnish: whipped cream or
   vanilla ice cream

Spray a 13"x9" baking pan with non-stick vegetable spray. Add pie filling and caramel topping; swirl mixture with a quick stir. Sprinkle dry cake mix evenly over the top; drizzle with melted butter. Bake at 350 degrees for 30 to 35 minutes. Let cool. Garnish portions with whipped cream or ice cream.

Lynda Robson, Boston, MA

Cherry Turnovers

These are so quick & easy, but taste like you spent hours in the kitchen making them!

Makes 8 turnovers

17-1/4 oz. pkg. frozen puff pastry,
   thawed
21-oz. can cherry pie filling, drained
1 c. powdered sugar
2 T. water

Separate puff pastry sheets and cut each into 4 squares. Divide pie filling evenly among squares. Brush pastry edges with water and fold in half diagonally. Seal and crimp edges with a fork. With a knife, make a small slit in tops of turnovers to vent. Bake on an ungreased baking sheet at 400 degrees for 15 to 18 minutes, until puffed and golden. Let cool slightly. Blend together powdered sugar and water; drizzle over warm turnovers.

Caramel Apple Pie Dump Cake

Becky Holsinger, Reedsville, OH

Easy Angel Food Bars

When I need a quick & easy dessert, I make these bars. As yummy as they are, people think they took a lot longer to make! Pineapple is my favorite, but you can use any kind of pie filling.

Makes 2 dozen

16-oz. pkg. angel food cake mix
21-oz. can cherry pie filling

Combine dry cake mix and pie filling; blend until smooth. Pour batter into an ungreased 15"x10" jelly-roll pan. Bake at 350 degrees for 20 to 25 minutes, until golden and top springs back when lightly touched. Cool in pan; cut into squares.

Micki Stephens, Marion, OH

Strawberry Pizza

With a sugar cookie crust, a cream cheese "sauce" and fresh strawberry topping, what's not to like about this dessert pizza? Be creative and add your favorite toppings like kiwi fruit, peach and banana slices and even chocolate curls.

Serves 6 to 8

18-oz. tube refrigerated sugar cookie dough
8-oz. pkg. cream cheese, softened
2 c. frozen whipped topping, thawed
1 t. vanilla extract
1 c. powdered sugar
12-3/4 oz. pkg. strawberry glaze
16-oz. pkg. strawberries, hulled and sliced

Roll out dough onto a greased 12" pizza pan; bake according to package directions. Let cool. In a large bowl, blend together cream cheese, whipped topping, vanilla and powdered sugar; spread over crust. Top with glaze and strawberries. Serve immediately, or cover and chill until serving time.

Easy Angel Food Bars

Vicki Echols, Corydon, KY

Speedy White Chocolate Fudge

Made in the microwave...so easy!

Makes about 2 dozen

8-oz. pkg. cream cheese, softened
4 c. powdered sugar
1-1/2 t. vanilla extract
12-oz. pkg. white chocolate chips
3/4 c. chopped pecans

In a large bowl, beat cream cheese with an electric mixer on low speed. Gradually add powdered sugar and vanilla; beat until smooth and set aside. Place chocolate chips in a microwave-safe bowl; microwave on high for one to two minutes, until melted. Stir chocolate until smooth; add cream cheese mixture and beat until smooth. Stir in pecans. Pour into a buttered 8"x8" baking pan. Chill until firm; cut into squares.

Pat Barbarita, Wilmington, DE

Lightning Bars

My mother, who passed away in 2010 at age 86, made these bar cookies all my life. My family still loves them. They are called Lightning Bars because they're so quick to make using ingredients always on hand. Every time I make them and share, everyone asks for the recipe. So delicious with a cup of coffee...enjoy!

Makes one dozen

1/2 c. butter, sliced
2 eggs
1 c. sugar
1 t. vanilla extract
1 t. baking powder
1/2 t. salt
1 c. all-purpose flour
3/4 c. chopped pecans, walnuts or almonds

Place butter in an 8"x8" baking pan; melt in a 350-degree oven and set aside. Beat eggs in a large bowl. Add sugar, vanilla, baking powder, salt and flour; mix well. Pour melted butter into batter; stir well. Pour batter into pan; sprinkle with nuts. Bake at 350 degrees for 20 to 30 minutes, until golden and a toothpick inserted in the center comes out clean. Cool completely; cut into squares.

Speedy White Chocolate Fudge

Jill Gagner, Morris, MN

E-Z Chocolate Chip Bars

Made from scratch in just a few minutes! My mom got this recipe from our neighbor when I was growing up. These crunchy bar cookies are always a big hit with my teens and their friends.

Makes one dozen

1 c. butter, softened
1 c. brown sugar, packed
1 t. vanilla extract
2 c. all-purpose flour
1 to 2 c. semi-sweet chocolate chips

Mix butter, brown sugar, vanilla and flour together in a bowl; stir in chocolate chips. Spread into a greased 12"x8" baking pan. Bake at 350 degrees for 20 to 25 minutes, until lightly golden. Cool; cut into squares.

Gladys Kielar, Whitehouse, OH

Better Than Brownies

If you love brownies, you'll like these baked goodies even better! These are so easy and always come out right. They are a favorite at our teacher staff meetings.

Makes about 2 dozen

3.4-oz. pkg. cook & serve chocolate
    pudding mix
2 c. milk
18-1/2 oz. pkg. chocolate cake mix
1 c. semi-sweet chocolate chips
1 c. chopped nuts

Prepare dry pudding mix with milk according to package directions; cook until slightly thickened. Remove from heat. Stir in dry cake mix. Spread batter in a greased 13"x9" baking pan; sprinkle with chocolate chips and nuts. Bake at 350 degrees for 30 minutes. Cool; cut into squares.

★ FANCY FINISH ★ Make your cookies a little bit fancy! Simply melt chocolate chips and butter together until the right consistency for dipping. Dip one-half of the cookie in the chocolate mixture and let sit on a sheet pan until the chocolate sets. Pretty!

E-Z Chocolate Chip Bars

Judy Taylor, Butler, MO

Morning Break
No-Bakes

I have made many less-than-successful attempts at chocolate no-bake cookies. At work on morning break, my co-workers were sharing helpful hints with me...I combined my recipe with their advice and haven't had a failure since!

Makes 2 dozen

1/2 c. butter
2 c. sugar
1/2 c. milk
3 to 4 T. baking cocoa
1 t. vanilla extract
3 c. quick-cooking oats, uncooked
1/2 c. creamy peanut butter

Combine butter, sugar, milk and 3 tablespoons cocoa in a heavy saucepan, using 4 tablespoons cocoa if a deeper chocolate flavor is desired. Over medium heat, bring mixture to a full boil; continue boiling for exactly 2 minutes. Remove from heat; stir in vanilla. Add oats and stir; add peanut butter and stir. Drop by heaping teaspoonfuls onto a wax paper-lined baking sheet; let stand until set.

★ TOAST IT ★ Make a good thing even better... add a little toasted coconut to your Morning Break No-Bakes! Spread shredded coconut on an ungreased baking sheet. Bake at 350 degrees for 7 to 12 minutes, stirring frequently, until toasted and golden.

Morning Break No-Bakes

Janice Schuler, Alburtis, PA

Sour Cherry Crumb Pie

We used to have a sour cherry tree in our backyard, so we made this pie often.

Serves 6 to 8

4 c. sour cherries, pitted
1/2 c. sour cherry juice
1 c. sugar
1/4 c. instant tapioca, uncooked
1/4 t. almond extract
1/8 t. salt
9-inch pie crust

Strain cherries in a colander, reserving 1/2 cup juice. In a bowl, combine cherries, reserved juice and remaining ingredients except crust. Mix well and spoon into unbaked crust. Bake at 400 degrees for 35 minutes. Remove pie from oven; sprinkle with Crumb Topping. Return to oven for 10 minutes, or until golden.

Crumb Topping:

1/3 c. butter, softened
2/3 c. sugar
1 c. all-purpose flour

Combine all ingredients; stir into a crumb consistency. Use immediately, or cover and refrigerate.

Cindy Lyzenga, Zeeland, MI

Brown Sugar Cake

This cake is easy and fun to make! It is always a hit at our church potlucks and I never take home any leftovers.

Makes 12 servings

18-1/2 oz. pkg. white cake mix
3.4-oz. pkg. instant vanilla pudding mix
2 eggs, beaten
2 c. milk
3/4 c. brown sugar, packed
3/4 c. semi-sweet chocolate chips

In a large bowl, stir together dry cake and pudding mixes, eggs and milk. Pour batter into a greased 13"x9" baking pan. Sprinkle brown sugar and chocolate chips over batter. Bake at 375 degrees for 30 to 35 minutes, until cake tests done with a toothpick.

Sour Cherry Crumb Pie

Marybeth Summers, Medford, OR

Luscious Strawberry Pie

A longtime family favorite. We have the best strawberries here in southern Oregon!

Makes 6 servings

4 c. strawberries, hulled and divided
8-inch pie crust, baked
3 T. cornstarch
1 c. sugar
1/4 t. salt
1 T. lemon juice
Garnish: whipped cream

Arrange half of the whole berries in baked pie crust; set aside. Crush remaining berries; place in a saucepan and add cornstarch, sugar and salt. Cook, stirring, over medium heat until thick and clear. Reduce heat and continue cooking for 10 minutes. Remove from heat; stir in lemon juice. Cool mixture completely; spoon over strawberries in pie crust. Garnish with whipped cream.

Laurel Perry, Loganville, GA

Dutch Apple Creamy Cobbler

A wonderful old-fashioned dessert.

Serves 6 to 8

1 c. graham cracker crumbs
3 T. butter, melted
14-oz. can sweetened condensed milk
1/4 c. lemon juice
8-oz. container sour cream
21-oz. can apple pie filling
3/4 c. chopped walnuts
1/2 t. cinnamon
1/4 t. nutmeg

In an 8"x8" baking pan, stir together cracker crumbs and melted butter with a fork. Press mixture down with fork to form a crust; set aside. In a bowl, stir together condensed milk and lemon juice; stir in sour cream. Spread condensed milk mixture over crust. Spoon pie filling over top. Bake at 400 degrees for 15 minutes, or until hot and bubbly. Combine walnuts and spices in a small bowl; sprinkle on top. Serve warm.

Luscious Strawberry Pie

Eileen Blass, Catawissa, PA

Peanut Butter-Chocolate Bars

Top with marshmallow creme for s'more fun!

Makes 25 to 30

1 c. creamy peanut butter
1/2 c. butter, melted
1 c. graham cracker crumbs
16-oz. pkg. powdered sugar
2 c. semi-sweet chocolate chips, melted

Combine first 4 ingredients together in a large mixing bowl; mix well using a wooden spoon. Press into the bottom of a well-greased 15"x10" jelly-roll pan; pour melted chocolate evenly over crust. Refrigerate for 15 minutes; score into bars but leave in pan. Refrigerate until firm; slice completely through scores and serve cold.

Dale Duncan, Waterloo, IA

Silver Moons

Your little werewolves will be howling for more!

Makes 8

1 T. sugar
1/4 t. cinnamon
16.3-oz. tube refrigerated large biscuits
1 c. apple pie filling
4 t. butter, melted
Garnish: powdered sugar

In a small bowl, combine sugar and cinnamon; set aside. Separate dough into 8 biscuits. Press each biscuit into a 5-inch circle. Arrange biscuits on greased baking sheets. Place 2 tablespoons pie filling on each circle half. Fold biscuits over filling; seal edges with a fork. Pierce each pie a few times with fork. Brush pies with melted butter and sprinkle with sugar mixture. Bake at 375 degrees for 15 to 20 minutes. Sprinkle with powdered sugar. Serve warm.

Peanut Butter-Chocolate Bars

Jacklyn Akey, Merrill, WI

Chocolatey Chewy Brownies

You'll love these chewy little squares of chocolate!

Makes about 2 dozen

1 c. butter, softened
2 c. sugar
4 eggs, beaten
1 c. all-purpose flour
4 1-oz. sqs. unsweetened baking
    chocolate, melted
1 c. chopped walnuts
Optional: powdered sugar

In a bowl, beat butter and sugar with an electric mixer on medium speed, until creamy. Beat in eggs, mixing well. Stir in remaining ingredients. Pour into a greased and floured 13"x9" baking pan. Bake at 350 degrees for 30 minutes. Cool. Dust with powdered sugar if desired. Cut into squares.

Beth Bundy, Long Prairie, MN

Brandon's Pumpkin Squares

My son Brandon loves anything with pumpkin in it...he requests this dessert all year 'round! His love for these bars makes them very special to me.

Makes 20 servings

12-oz. can evaporated milk
3 eggs, beaten
2 t. pumpkin pie spice
1/2 t. salt
1 c. sugar
15-oz. can pumpkin
181/2-oz. pkg. yellow cake mix
1/2 c. butter, sliced
Garnish: whipped topping

Combine all ingredients except cake mix, butter and garnish. Pour into a greased 13"x11" pan. Sprinkle with dry cake mix; do not stir. Dot with butter. Bake at 350 degrees for 30 to 35 minutes. Serve with whipped topping.

★ SIMPLE SWAP ★ Out of unsweetened baking chocolate? Just replace each square of unsweetened baking chocolate with 3 level tablespoons of cocoa plus one tablespoon of vegetable oil.

Chocolatey Chewy Brownies

Michelle Sheridan, Columbus, OH

Strawberry-Yogurt Mousse

A very easy-to-make, refreshing dessert I've made for many years... you'll love it!

Makes 10 servings

2 8-oz. containers strawberry yogurt
1/2 c. strawberries, hulled and
   crushed
8-oz. container frozen light whipped
   topping, thawed

Combine yogurt and strawberries; mix well. Fold in whipped topping; blend well. Spoon into cups or glasses. Place in refrigerator for 30 minutes before serving.

Bonnie Allar, Santa Rosa, CA

Peach Cobbler Cupcakes

My most-requested muffin-like cupcakes...my family & friends love them! They disappear right away whenever I make them to share. We like them with a cup of hot tea.

Makes 1-1/2 dozen

3 c. all-purpose flour
1 c. sugar
1-1/2 T. baking soda
1/2 t. salt
3/4 c. butter, diced
1-3/4 c. milk
15-oz. can sliced peaches, drained
   and chopped
Optional: 6 t. brown sugar, packed

Mix flour, sugar, baking soda and salt in a large bowl. Cut in butter with a pastry blender or a fork. Add milk and peaches; stir just until moistened. Spoon batter into 18 greased muffin cups, filling 2/3 full. Add one teaspoon of brown sugar into the center of each cupcake if desired. Bake at 400 degrees for 15 to 20 minutes, until golden. Turn out and cool slightly on a wire rack; serve warm or cooled.

Strawberry-Yogurt Mousse

Nancy Willis, Farmington Hills, MI

Easy Apple Crisp

Garnish with a dollop of whipped cream and a dusting of cinnamon... yummy!

Serves 12 to 14

4 c. apples, cored and sliced
1/2 c. brown sugar, packed
1/2 c. quick-cooking oats, uncooked
1/3 c. all-purpose flour
3/4 t. cinnamon
1/4 c. butter
Garnish: whipped cream,
   cinnamon, apple slices

Arrange apple slices in a greased 11"x8" baking pan; set aside. Combine oats, flour, cinnamon and butter; stir until crumbly and sprinkle over apples. Bake at 350 degrees for 30 to 35 minutes. Garnish as desired.

Jill Ball, Highland, UT

Sweet Apple Tarts

I like to use Granny Smith apples in these tarts, but you can use any good baking apple that you like. Everyone loves it for our Christmas dessert.

Makes 9 servings

1 sheet frozen puff pastry, thawed
1/2 c. apricot jam
4 Granny Smith apples, peeled,
   cored and very thinly sliced
1/4 c. brown sugar, packed
1/2 t. cinnamon
1/2 c. pistachio nuts, chopped
Optional: vanilla ice cream

Roll pastry into a 12-inch square on a lightly floured surface. Cut pastry into nine 3-inch squares. Arrange squares on an ungreased baking sheet; pierce with a fork. Spoon jam evenly over each square; arrange apple slices over jam. Combine brown sugar and cinnamon in a small bowl; mix well. Sprinkle over apple slices. Bake at 400 degrees for 20 to 25 minutes, until pastry is golden and apples are crisp-tender. Sprinkle with nuts. Serve warm topped with scoops of ice cream, if desired.

Easy Apple Crisp

Henry Burnley, Ankeny, IA

Brownie Buttons

These little bits of chocolate, caramel and peanut butter will be the sweet goodie they ask for again and again.

Makes 20

16-oz. pkg. refrigerated mini brownie bites dough
11-oz. pkg. assorted mini peanut butter cup candies and chocolate-coated caramels

Spray mini muffin cups with non-stick vegetable spray. Spoon brownie dough evenly into each cup, filling almost full. Bake at 350 degrees for 19 to 20 minutes. Cool in pans 3 to 4 minutes; gently press a candy into each baked brownie until top of candy is level with top of brownie. Cool 10 minutes in pans. Gently twist each brownie to remove from pan. Cool on a wire rack.

Debra Boyd, Gibsonia, PA

Peanut Butter Brownies

These are my kids' favorite treats. I always used to make them for camping and picnics. Even though my kids now are in their twenties and are on their own, from time to time they still ask me to make them a pan of these yummy brownies!

Makes 2 dozen

1/2 c. creamy peanut butter
1/4 c. butter, softened
1 t. vanilla extract
1 c. brown sugar, packed
2 eggs
2/3 c. all-purpose flour

Blend together peanut butter, butter, vanilla and brown sugar. Add eggs, one at a time, beating well after each addition. Stir in flour. Spread batter evenly in a well-greased 8"x8" baking pan. Bake at 350 degrees for 20 to 30 minutes, until center tests done with a toothpick. Do not overbake. Cool; cut into bars.

★ TASTY TWIST ★ A scrumptious dessert for crumbly brownies or bar cookies! In stemmed glasses, alternate layers of ice cream and crumbled brownies. Garnish with whipped topping and a sprinkle of chopped nuts...no one will ever know the difference.

Brownie Buttons

Melonie Klosterho, Fairbanks, AK

Easy Cherry Cobbler

If they're available, use fresh-from-the-farm pitted cherries for a special treat.

Makes 8 servings

15-oz. can tart red cherries
1 c. all-purpose flour
1 c. sugar, divided
1 c. 2% milk
2 t. baking powder
1/8 t. salt
1/4 c. butter, melted
Optional: vanilla ice cream or
   whipped topping

Bring cherries with juice to a boil in a saucepan over medium heat; remove from heat. Mix flour, 3/4 cup sugar, milk, baking powder and salt in a medium bowl. Pour butter into 6 one-cup ramekins or into a 2-quart casserole dish; pour flour mixture over butter. Add cherries; do not stir. Sprinkle remaining sugar over top. Bake at 400 degrees for 20 to 30 minutes. Serve warm with ice cream or whipped cream, if desired.

★ DID YOU KNOW? ★ Canned fruit pie filling is different from canned fruit in syrup... be sure to double-check which kind is called for in cobbler & crisp recipes.

Easy Cherry Cobbler

Dueley Lucas, Somerset, KY

Oh-So-Easy Peach Cobbler

Wonderful topped with vanilla ice cream or a splash of milk... or even all by itself!

Serves 10 to 12

2 15-oz. cans sliced peaches, drained and 1/2 c. juice reserved
1/2 c. butter, sliced
1 c. self-rising flour
1 c. sugar
1 c. milk

Arrange peaches in a 13"x9" baking pan that has been sprayed with non-stick vegetable spray. Pour in reserved juice. Arrange butter slices over peaches; set aside. In a bowl, mix flour, sugar and milk, stirring until smooth. Spoon batter over peaches, spreading to the edges of pan. Bake at 375 degrees for 30 minutes, or until golden. Serve warm.

Mary Jackson, Fishers, IN

Bragging-Rights Banana Pudding

This recipe was handed down from my wonderful mother-in-law. It is a definite crowd-pleaser!

Makes 15 servings

5-1/4-oz. pkg. instant vanilla pudding mix
3 c. 2 % milk
16-oz. container sour cream
12-oz. container frozen whipped topping, thawed
10-oz. pkg. vanilla wafers, divided
4 bananas, sliced and divided

In a bowl, with an electric mixer on low speed, beat dry pudding mix and milk for 2 to 3 minutes, until thickened. Beat in sour cream; fold in topping. Set aside several vanilla wafers. In a large deep bowl, layer half each of remaining wafers, bananas and pudding mixture. Repeat layering. Crush reserved wafers and sprinkle on top. Cover; chill until served.

Oh-So-Easy Peach Cobbler

Index

U. S. to Metric Recipe Equivalents

Volume Measurements

¼ teaspoon	1 mL
½ teaspoon	2 mL
1 teaspoon	5 mL
1 tablespoon = 3 teaspoons	15 mL
2 tablespoons = 1 fluid ounce	30 mL
¼ cup	60 mL
⅓ cup	75 mL
½ cup = 4 fluid ounces	125 mL
1 cup = 8 fluid ounces	250 mL
2 cups = 1 pint = 16 fluid ounces	500 mL
4 cups = 1 quart	1 L

Weights

1 ounce	30 g
4 ounces	120 g
8 ounces	225 g
16 ounces = 1 pound	450 g

Baking Pan Sizes

Square

8x8x2 inches	2 L = 20x20x5 cm
9x9x2 inches	2.5 L = 23x23x5 cm

Rectangular

13x9x2 inches	3.5 L = 33x23x5 cm

Loaf

9x5x3 inches	2 L = 23x13x7 cm

Round

8x1-1/2 inches	1.2 L = 20x4 cm
9x1-1/2 inches	1.5 L = 23x4 cm

Recipe Abbreviations

t. = teaspoon	ltr. = liter
T. = tablespoon	oz. = ounce
c. = cup	lb. = pound
pt. = pint	doz. = dozen
qt. = quart	pkg. = package
gal. = gallon	env. = envelope

Oven Temperatures

300° F	150° C
325° F	160° C
350° F	180° C
375° F	190° C
400° F	200° C
450° F	230° C

Kitchen Measurements

A pinch = ⅛ tablespoon
1 fluid ounce = 2 tablespoons
3 teaspoons = 1 tablespoon
4 fluid ounces = ½ cup
2 tablespoons = ⅛ cup
8 fluid ounces = 1 cup
4 tablespoons = ¼ cup
16 fluid ounces = 1 pint
8 tablespoons = ½ cup
32 fluid ounces = 1 quart
16 tablespoons = 1 cup
16 ounces net weight = 1 pound
2 cups = 1 pint
4 cups = 1 quart
4 quarts = 1 gallon